VISUALISING RESILIENT COMMUNITIES

MOHAMED BUHEJI

authorHOUSE®

AuthorHouse™ UK
1663 Liberty Drive
Bloomington, IN 47403 USA
www.authorhouse.co.uk
Phone: 0800 047 8203 (Domestic TFN)
       +44 1908 723714 (International)

Published by AuthorHouse 02/29/2020

ISBN: 978-1-7283-9928-7 (sc)
ISBN: 978-1-7283-9927-0 (e)

CONTENTS

PREFACE - WHY TO VISUALISE RESILIENT COMMUNITIES?

Introduction

The world is full of challenges. These challenges have a repetitive trend which is turning into a crisis. Hence, each community need to be able to either early foresight and identify a crisis or have a sustained ability to mitigate challenges through being more tolerant and resilient.

Being more resilient helps to create lasting change, which is what differentiates any community outcome or realized change. Therefore, the purpose of this work is to create aspiring leaders from around the world who have the right mindset and passion towards creating a difference towards this challenging, positive change. Resilient driven communities' leaders need to build the capacity for focusing on specific rising needs that can be used to changing the mindset of their followers. This initiative could produce pragmatic problem-solving communities that can take action or be confident to embrace the unknown.

While the literature is full of community resilience case studies, techniques and tools that were developed over the years, there is a clear gap in the body of knowledge about how to create resilient communities before any crisis occurs which would have the capacity to mitigate any current or coming risks. As mentioned in Buheji (2018 and 2017), this needs types of community engagement projects that help such a community to adapt to change and minimize the impact of any crisis.

Creating such resilient communities enhance their capacity to focus on the big-picture. History shows that having clarity of what differentiates any community to deliver exceptional business expertise even during the time of crisis would make such community be more prepared to deal with intractable problems while remaining focused on its long-term goals.

Importance of Visualising the Desired Resilient Communities

Visualisation helps to improve our focused reflection on any desired change. To solve any socio-economic challenge, we need to visualise it from all perspectives. Tackling complex problems or sudden changes need mechanisms, and that ensure suitable resources.

Govaerts et al. (2010) seen that once we start any change with clear intention through visualisation of the outcome, we could be more ready for sudden challenges. Visualisation helps us to specify the type of knowledge collected and thus start waves of empathetic thinking. This is suitable for building resilient communities that can have differentiated interpretations which involve dealing with ideal qualities that proactively handle turbulent and risky experiences.

Visualisation is highly related to the capacity of achieving habits of expectation structure that is created in the brain as storage of bins in the memory. Govaerts et al. (2010) seen that once we start the intention through visualising what the outcome should be, as the intention of having more resilient communities in the world, we actually start the process of searching for defined specific meanings. In our case, the meaning would be what is the specific mechanisms of change. These meanings lead to building specific awareness that direct the journey for a specific type of knowledge collection.

In this book, we could focus on the following types of knowledge collection that construct our focused intentions towards more resilient economies and communities. The first type of knowledge collection focus on the need to raise our commitment to exploring the best approaches and mechanisms that address the rising need for resilient economies and communities. Different mitigation techniques are retrieved so that communities would be more equipped to turn the coming socio-economic, or environmental, or socio-political problems and the challenges to success stories and models of reference.

Framework Proposed to Visualise and Realise Resilient Communities

In order to effectively visualise and realise more resilient communities, we need to be selective on the type of knowledge collection that focuses on how the challenges would help in inspiring the targeted community or creating a difference to its ability to be more tolerant, or to be able to bounce back. Therefore, this book proposes the following theoretical framework that could help to visualise and then realise the targeted resilient communities. As shown in Figure (0-1) the reader could visualise how communities could learn how to mitigate risks, enhance their inspiring and selective productivity, becomes more agile to socio-economic problem solving, know how to exploits their hidden assets of wealth and finally can be transformed to be outcome-driven communities.

To reach the levels set by the framework proposed in Figure (0-1), communities need to be engaged with socio-economic projects that transform them towards having more resilient mindset, which focuses on being or staying self-sufficient, follows proactive and reactive approaches, while absorbing sudden shocks and engineering their empathy to be stronger and available in the right time and place. The framework targets also to strengthen the communities confidence in their capacity to visualise their resilience and be prepared for the worse. Also, the editor claims it is with such framework communities could develop and thrive through finding opportunities inside the problem.

Figure (0-1) Framework proposed to Visualise and then Realise More Resilient Communities

The ultimate goal of this book is to create readers that would develop or adopt similar models that bring more resilient communities that maintain and further inspire the world towards better humanity stages. Please start visualising!

Reference

Buheji, M (2018) Understanding the Power of Resilience Economy: An Inter-Disciplinary Perspective to Change the World Attitude to Socio-Economic Crisis, AuthorHouse, UK.

Buheji, M and Ahmed, D (2017) Breaking the Shield-Introduction to Inspiration Engineering: Philosophy, Practices and Success Stories, Archway Publishing, FROM SIMON & SCHUSTER, USA.

PART ONE

THE RISING NEED FOR RESILIENT ECONOMIES AND COMMUNITIES

UNDERSTANDING MEANING OF 'RESILIENCE'[1]

As per Andrew Zolli and Ann Healy

[1]Buheji, M (2015) Book Review 'Resilience' for Andrew Zolli and Ann Healy, Journal of Inspiration Economy, Vol 2, Issue.1, pp. 121-126.

Introduction – Why Review this book?

"Life is a process of becoming. A combination of states we have to go through. Where people fail is that they wish to elect a state and remain in it. This is a kind of death." Anais Nin. The 'Resilience' book takes us through a journey we need in our current era that is having the characteristics or practices or striving towards "resilience". The book re-introduced the word and the concept of "Resilience" to the knowledge community in a time where we need such an inspiration. More than ever, before the practice and results of "Resilience" is highly needed to create or even restore all the inspirational deeds that need to be our world societies to flourish and compete.

As an innovation practitioner and professional writers, both Andrew Zolli and Ann Healy produced for the world a comprehensive review of the types of resilience we need to visualize and work for a better life. The 'Resilience' book of Zolli and Healy (2012) takes you as a book in many forms of potential inspiration if we relook about the nature of life or refocus how life is taking us towards more demand for being more resilient. Zolli and Healy researched resilience needs in every aspect of life, from global warming to world financial systems. Luckily, a new book claims to discover the key to bouncing back.

Meaning and Definition of the Word Resilient

The British dictionary defines resilience for an object or material as being "capable of regaining original shape or position after bending, stretching, or being compressed, or other deformation". While resilience for a person was defined for the British dictionary or community as recovering easily and quickly from shock, illness, hardship.

The word "resilience" thus means the ability to spring back or rebound or even return to the original form or position after being bent or been compressed, or stretched. Therefore "Resilience" can be seen in recovering readily from war, illness, depression, adversity. A person or an organisation or a society who described with the resilience they are more of buoyant and flexible enough not break.

Zolli and Healy (2013) defined resilience as the ability to dynamically react to the unexpected, to patch up holes as they appear to keep things from spiralling out of control.

Resilience Importance to an Inspired World Economy

OECD (2013) reports that in the last two years, the concept of "resilience" has achieved significant attention on the international stage, due to the seen trends of growing risks caused by violence, conflicts, climate change, disasters, global shocks, urbanisation and ageing populations which are all considered to be inter-connected in being a source of the world instability and turbulence.

As per the OECD literature review, having the concept of resilience established in our society's emphasis that working in silos no longer makes sense if we are to deal with these risks properly. Therefore, OECD calls all the social development actors, and even states leaders will need to work more closely together.

Zolli and Healy raise the need to work collaboratively and holistically today more than ever. The authors 'resilience' examples in different situations seen of why do things go wrong and what can be done to fix them. The authors tried to discover Resilience: Why things bounce back and then came with vital themes that can be applied to our needs of an inspired world economy.

How can "resilience" help an inspiration economy world, a question I was looking an answer for in Zolli's and Healy's book review. I have to admit that even though I found some of the answers, the book couldn't address the 'how' as much as addressing the 'what' of 'Resilience'. However, the Zolli's and Healy's arguments did have an impact on my understanding of what connects all the types of instability we experience in our life, but I was not confident of how to create this resilience practically in our societies. Therefore, one could say that further research is needed in addressing 'how' to create a resilient situation or resilient society or economy, or even in this matter, resilient spirit (Lopez, 2010).

After finishing the first review of the book, I was more inspired towards the need to work more focused on initiatives that would connect the different communities of the world and the different specialities to address such an important issue and also to consider the keyword 'resilience' to be part of Journal of Inspiration Economy main keywords. Actually, 'Resilience' as a word has the potential to bring together scientists, practitioners, humanitarians, development actors to work together on issues as societies conflicts, disaster planning, conflict mitigation, social or economic development and most of all social acceptance or co-existence. Yes, after reading the book and did my research, I can see how 'Resilience' has an inspirational edge to let us join forces of multi-disciplined game-changers or change agents that would build new layers in our communities and establish research clusters that would deliver more focused efforts to transform our goodwill into better working practices on the ground.

Resilient Organisations

In understanding the 'Resilience' book of Zolli and Healy (2013) one can appreciate many wrong practices around us today, such as seeing really how organisations, people and societies complicate systems designs to the extent when things go wrong, it will lead to a series of failures that nearly cause total collapse, similar to the latest world financial crisis. Zolli and Healy did a great job in showing us how resilience can play a major role through examples as overcoming the poisoned wells in Bangladesh to the cases of coral-reef preservation efforts in Jamaica.

One has really to pause as the analogy of both Zolli and Healy in using a car approaching a cliff when talking about the major challenges facing human civilization. The authors believe that we live in a world of connected cliffs, i.e. an ecological cliff is believed to be connected to the economic cliff, which is connected to the social cliff, which is connected to the technological cliff. A disruption in one could, like a bunch of steers on a rope line, pull everybody all over." Therefore, resilience here would focus on mitigation of the damages that might occur to any of the cliffs.

Thus the book focuses on adaptability.

Zolli and Healy (2013) believe that we can come with systems more resilient in general when we empower individuals, communities, small groups of actors. I,e, Resilience might occur because of inspiration and/or inspiration might occur because of the presence of resilience. While resilient organizations do have some level of the hierarchy, says Zolli, the best way to maximize resiliency is to employ a networked, decentralized approach that empowers actors to attack problems.

The resilience that is not covered
in Zolli and Healy (2013)

The book Zolli and Healy (2013) has comprehensively covered the concept of resilience from all angles, except for how it can be planted or transferred in our lives, our families and our community. In other words, I felt the book didn't address well How to become more resilient. Therefore, one can argue that the book doesn't give enough inspiration if people want to have their communities and families future to be stable with co-existence and full of harmony (Namka,2014). Social resilience means that our communities must be taught or even challenged on how to compromise between what is taught in schools with what is not taught in schools; especially in the concept of resilience. Today with depression and society disorders are increasing in our societies, the skills of resilience need to be discussed in more detail.

In a study published by the author, students who had the chance to work in helping society through, i.e. NGOs or even their teams in schools found to be happier than others with the same conditions, but without such the contribution, so, resilience can be created through certain conditions or environment.

The resilience book Zolli and Healy (2013) couldn't also cover the types of natural enablers that support the presence of the ability to bounce back. For example, it more and more published today that researchers are studying the role of certain genes and hormones that enhance depression or minimize the human ability to bounce back (Wicks, 2010). Therefore, the psychologist Elizabeth Lombardo (2009) believes that resilience should be defined as "realistic optimism, hardiness, determination, and self-confidence". The *Proceedings of the National Academy of Sciences (2009) also revealed that* families with a history of depression, i.e. low resilience found to have a significantly thinner right cortex, or outer surface of the brain which affected their memory abilities.

Resilience and meditation found to play a great role in enhancing those ruminating thoughts about the difficulties of life by making us focus on something else—mindfulness. Though experts differ on whether resilience can be developed as an adult, many believe it can go through practices similar to meditation. Our "explanatory style" and how we deal with things of being happy and optimistic, also found to play a role in our ability to bounce back and stay resilient (Free Press, 1998). How we look at things positively in life found to alleviate our pleasures in life, or allow us to live fully. Different types of meditation found to reduce the level of pessimism and to believe in a permanent and never-ending bad situation (Wicks, 2010).

Resilience then is not the same as becoming unrealistically always sweet; it the opposite in a way that it makes you become more realistic about what's happening in your life. However, these tools that create resilience like anything requires practice and repetition.

To be resilient means you have to capitalize on your strength. In a large-scale study done by the Andrew Shatte (2002) author of *The Resilience Factor, it was found that* resilience capability of both men and women are equal. However, women are less convinced of their skill problem-solving. Resilience requires the practice of breaking down a problem into parts, then determining which one you can solve.

Resilience as A Symptom of Inspired People.

Thomas Edison is a good example of a resilience personality. History proves that such resilient characters are most prone to survive challenges (Minton, 2010). Names as Abraham Lincoln, Henry Ford, Walt Disney, shows that inspired people never give up and keep trying till the last moment and that what makes them more resilient. History shows that such a resilient spirit prevents such legends from labelling themselves as a failure and instead shift them to learn from mistakes towards making more better lifetime judgments or directions (Pulley and Wakefield, 2003). Such resilient people see any predicament as temporary, and their mindset always looks forward towards success.

Inspired people spend more time focusing on their strengths and have a unique ability to bounce back with all the setbacks and move forward. Resilient people are also very good at stopping to learn from their mistakes (Reivich and Shatte, 2003).

Resilience, therefore, is a trait that can be built through reframing our mindsets and through trying continuously to look at the situation from different angles and letting go of ego control. This type of ability, i.e. the ability to continuously reframe our mindset, make us more resilient not to react emotionally to anything unless we decide to. Such resilience becomes more of a habit from continuously building the ability to gain a new perspective, through being open to ideas while detaching yourself the situation.

Then a new plan on how to proceed or to overcome a failure can lead up to bounce back towards embracing a new path and focus (Everly et. Al., 2010).

Final Remarks

Resilience by Zolli and Healy (2013) is a well-structured, well research book the used holistic approach to introducing the concept of resilience to the knowledge community. However, the review of this book shows that Zolli and Healy (2013) didn't cover in their scope enough material about the role of 'experiential learning' that would help to create more resilient spirit (Lopez, 2010). Also, the book doesn't have active interventions on how to create resilience.

If we believe that resilience can be developed, we need to utilize more tools that would make it spread in our societies forever. Resilience another discovery of a natural inspiration mechanism that is available and accessible to all humanity no matter who they are or what they are.

Reference

Anonymous (2011) *Inspiration and Resilience Motivational video*, http://www.youtube.com/watch?v=sJROplAvZzU&spfreload=1

Anonymous (2014) Building Resilience: the EU's approach. European Commission, Humanitarian Aid and Civil Protection Development and Cooperation http://ec.europa.eu/echo/files/aid/countries/factsheets/thematic/resilience_en.pdf

Anonymous (2013) *The Oregon Resilience Plan*, Save Lives, Preserve Our Communities and Our Economy, Report to the 77th Legislative Assembly from Oregon Seismic Safety Policy Advisory Commission Salem, Oregon. http://www.oregon.gov/OMD/OEM/osspac/docs/Oregon_Resilience_Plan_draft_Executive_Summary.pdf. Accessed on: 1/1/2014.

Anonymous (2013) *Building Resilience in Supply Chains, World Economic Forum*, http://www3.weforum.org/docs/WEF_RRN_MO_BuildingResilienceSupplyChains_Report_2013.pdf. Accessed on: 1/1/2014.

Boniwell, I (2014) *Educating For Happiness and Resilience*, TEDxHull, http://www.youtube.com/watch?v=DbC18wFkHNI, Accessed on: 1/1/2014.

Everly, G; Strouse, D and Everly, G (2010) *The Secrets of Resilient Leadership: When Failure Is Not an Option; Six Essential Skills for Leading through Adversity.* New York: DiaMedica, pp.152.

Lopez, Todd (2010) Soldiers Learning to 'Bounce Back' with Resilience Training. *Soldiers* 65, no. 2 (Feb): 19

Minton, E (2010) *Resiliency and Post-Traumatic Growth.* Officer 86, no. 1 (Feb/March): pp. 32-33. ProQuest

Namka, L (2014) Teaching Resilience to Children, http://angriesout.com/resilience.pdf. Accessed on: 1/1/2014.

Namka, L (2014) The Road to Resilience, the American Psychological Association, http://helpcenter.apa.org/files/The-Road-to-Resilience.pdf. Accessed on: 1/1/2014.

OECD (2013) What does "resilience" mean for donors? file:///C:/Users/Buhiji/Desktop/May%2010%202013%20FINAL%20resilience%20PDF.pdf, Accessed: 21/11/2014

Pulley, M and Wakefield, M (2003) Building Resiliency: How to Thrive in Times of Change. Rev. ed. Greensboro: Center for Creative Leadership, pp. 26.

Reivich, K and Shatte. A (2003) *The Resilience Factor: 7 Keys to Finding Your Inner Strength and Overcoming Life's Hurdles.* New York: Broadway Books, 342pp.

Wicks, R (2010) *Bounce: Living the Resilient Life.* New York: Oxford University Press, pp. 218.

REVIEWING 'HOW CAPITALISM IS DESTROYING ITSELF?'

Technology Displaced by Financial Innovation2

[2]Buheji, M and Ahmed, D (2019) Reviewing 'How Capitalism is Destroying Itself?' Technology Displaced by Financial Innovation, American Journal of Economics, Vol. 9, Issue 5, pp. 264-267.

Abstract

This paper reviews the work of William Kingston (2017) published by Elgar. Kingston shows how capitalism has exhausted all the inherited moral values. The researchers of this review evaluate this work and compare it to previous work, starting from Ibn-Khaldun until how the latest different economies emerged and then destroyed itself.

The paper focuses on the literature emphasis on how capitalism being under threats of destruction and what are signs of Transformation from capitalism. A comparison of Kingston's and other authors are made on how they see capitalism is destroying itself. The paper concludes with implications on the current destruction of capitalism and lessons learned.

Keywords: Capitalism, Economy, Transformation from Capitalism, New Economies.

1.0   Introduction

Ibn-Khaldun, confirms that none of the economies has continued, they all went into death. The famous cycle of Ibn-Khaldun discusses how different economies would emerge and then destroyed, although some stay for longer. This coincides with the speed of the new economies that are coming faster than before, such as knowledge economy and behavioural economy, as inspiration economy, Buheji (2016). However, Ibn-Khaldun and others believe that deformation of the purpose of the uprising, development and growth of any economy and its length of survival depends on the amount of trust it continues to gain amongst the continuously generating societies. In relevance to these theories, Kingston (2017) focused on identifying how capitalism is going through self-destruction through losing its trust. Today, many people refer to capitalism as a form of individualism that uses domination techniques, like property rights, to address self-interest, with some public benefit.

2.0   Literature Review

2.1   Emphasis on the literature of Capitalism Being Under Threats of Destruction

More than ever now, capitalism is speeding its destruction of itself through the laws underwriting economic and financial innovation, supported by what claimed to democracy which gradually captured and shaped by those who could benefit most from them. This book shows that the outcome is a reduced ability to generate real wealth combined with exceptional inequality.

Joseph Schumpeter (1942) seen that capitalist society would be destroyed by its own success, due to the growing hostility of the institutions of a free society to the freedom of speech. The entrepreneurial market economy, on the other hand, loses the source of its wealth, and becomes hostile to the extent the society forgets how fragile the market economy is.

2.2 Signs of Transformation from Capitalism

Studies show that any capital-based transformation requires the accumulation of wealth. With this reality of wealth accumulation, the intellectual class of the society also need to be actively fit to free-market hostility created by the institutions. Once society ultimately rests on the wealth of the entrepreneurs of the growing class, who are mostly disconnected from real market competition, capitalism starts to fail.

Formal school and university graduates are another sign of market vulnerability. These youths become anti-market bias practices bring in anti-liberal ideology and make them turned against the ideals of a free society. Once the educational system fails to accommodate the realized benefits of the thriving marketplace, youth become the early movers of the entire economic system in society.

The other early sign of transformation from capitalism is when a collection of the community starts to believe that the system undervalues their capacity and know-how. We can live another transformation from capitalism when we experience the rapid increase of the unemployed. The unemployed society members generally go psychologically through a discontent mind that breeds resentment and end up with a utilitarian society that is full of social criticism.

Finally, the transformation from capitalism can be experienced in the inequality caused by the financiers that are used to escape from the laws so that they continue to generate money from nothing.

2.3 How Capitalism is Destroying itself?

Capitalism, as we know it today, is becoming a matter of wealth-seeking and -redistribution rather than a matter that creates a quality of life for the majority of the community. More and more entrepreneurs are becoming isolated from the profit and loss test of the market and started to lose touch with the division of labour and its philosophy of innovation and wealth creation. This leads the curve of capitalism to sharply drops down.

Capitalism is an economy today that is dumping its liabilities on the youth and the future generation. Its current growth depends on intergenerational theft. Capitalism lost much of its capacity to increase the productivity of economic activity and the workings of modern financial systems.

Capitalism clearly is in bad shape if cannot keep hiring workers, or creating an equality-based entrepreneurial culture with enough labour income, enough consumer confidence, enough consumption and enough final demand.

Shifting income from labour to capital without having an excess capacity and a lack of aggregate demand found to create also threats on capitalism. For the current capitalism to thrive, it needs to push labour costs more and more down, but labour costs are someone else's income and consumption. Hence this creates status self-destruction.

Capitalism will destroy itself if it manages to create a massive redistribution of income from labour to capital, from wages to profits. This again increases the inequality of income. Also, the dangers of capitalism out fold when we have the household expenditure higher than the marginal returns from a firm. The reason capitalism eventually would fail is that the system is built to protect the concentration of wealth over time.

2.4 What is happening to the Capital Economy today?

The economic reality makes it inevitable that the capitalists focus on reducing labour costs. This is done today more with the automation of jobs. Notice that the very workers who were the beneficiaries of capitalism in the previous stage are now losing their jobs thanks to it.

Capitalists find it more prudent to pay overseas workers a fraction of the cost. This allows them to stay more competitive. However, notice the fact that the high wage earned by workers was the very basis of the market! If high wages are eliminated, the capitalists inadvertently shoot themselves in the foot. Over a period of time, fall in wages manifests in the form of a slowdown or a recession.

This is the stage wherein capitalists are desperate to find more sales to keep the momentum going, hence manage to come up with short-term solutions to the current community problems. These solutions inevitably generate growth and creation of credit. This results in workers who no longer have jobs that can enable them to buy products while they are in debt.

Due to the job market is shrinking, the bad debts of the general population are increasing. This makes the unemployed to try to make money via a mortgage. Such a mortgage crisis is only a result of the system that made it exist. The capitalism approach today to such problems is constrained by introducing bailout packages, and rising wages of workers, which amplify the problem in many developed and emerging economies with high populations like China and India.

3.0 Synthesis and Implications of 'How Capitalism is Destroying Itself?'

The book deals with capitalism in relevance to economic cycles and practically mentions how this affects both the micro- and macro-economic outcome of any community. Although Kingston (2017) explains briefly how capitalism could avoid its current disadvantages, he did not introduce the new economies have more advantages that capitalism could benefit from.

Structurally the book is full of quotes, which make it not very interesting for none specialists on the subject. It is a collective book about the subject rather a research with clear field studies.

Clearly, Kingston (2017) relies on the longstanding opinions of Marx, Schumpeter and Minsky, specifically on the development of financial innovation which has replaced the technological innovation. Kingston's sees 'free-market economy' destroying the economic fabric of society.

As capitalism is based on the assumptions that a great a share of the world's resources could be bought, i.e. lands and natural resources could be brought regardless of who might be deprived. Finally, in a capitalist economy, we have all the opportunity to make something of ourselves.

4.0 Discussion and Conclusion

Capitalism has benefits. However, the point of Kingston (2017) is that these benefits do not always reach the consumers and much of it goes to the wealthiest. The reviewed book in this paper paints a clear picture of the increased risks of coming recessions in the near future before capitalism goes down. The author nicely organises the chapters towards understanding the history of capitalism and how it was developed. Then Kingston (2017) focus on the market power and the role of wealth dominated by money. Then concludes with a discussion of how capitalism could be saved.

An essential aspect of this is that entrepreneurs and "the rich" are blamed for the downsides of the business cycle. Even these entrepreneurs are increasingly blamed for the growing frequency and severity of these risks. Marx had predicted a long time ago that these risks and series of crashes could wipe out entire institutions and pose a systemic risk to the capitalist system.

Capitalism requires justice to survive; this "justice" is represented today by unearned wealth. This type of behaviour makes capitalism like a game of monopoly where most of the money and property is concentrated into the hands of very few, and those few can pass those holdings on to their offspring, it is unlikely that wealth ever moves to lower concentrations.

In order to stop the destruction, capitalism needs to focus on realised productivity rather than focusing on concentrating wealth with the few. Unless this move happens, we would continue to experience stories about the persistent concentration of wealth with the few, due to many bureaucratic red tapes as the unsatisfactory regulation and forced interventions of the rich dominating people towards to entrepreneurial start-ups. This does not help to close seen income inequality, which is increasing with time.

Karl Marx predicted the coming crisis of capitalism, which he believed it is like slavery and feudalism. This is because of the conflicting forces inherent in capitalism, which Marx called 'problems internal contradictions. Capitalism supposed to provide a better standard of living for the entire society for both the working class and the investors.

Finally, one could conclude that William Kingston (2017) set a truthful and honest question, even when are many are hostile to it. To answer this question without bias, we need to bring all the capitalists and their opponents and create a tolerant environment for discussion. This is the purpose of this paper.

References

Buheji, M (2016) Handbook of Inspiration Economy. Bookboon.

Buheji, M (2019) Industrial Relations in Emerging Economies, A book Review. American Journal of Economics, 9(1): 21-22.

Schumpeter, J (1942) Capitalism, Socialism, and Democracy (1942). University of Illinois at Urbana-Champaign's Academy for Entrepreneurial Leadership Historical Research Reference in Entrepreneurship.

https://papers.ssrn.com/sol3/papers.cfm?abstract_id=1496200 Accessed on: 1/6/2019

William Kingston (2017) 'How Capitalism is Destroying Itself?', Technology Displaced by Financial Innovation. Elgar, UK.

THE ECONOMICS OF CLIMATE – RESILIENT DEVELOPMENT[3]

[3]Buheji, M. (2018) The Economics of Climate-Resilient Development – A Book Review, Applied Finance and Accounting Vol. 4, No. 2, pp. 29-30.

Abstract

Future foresight specialists have been warning about the influence of climate change on many coming socio-economic crises. Climate change requires different resilient communities beyond their previous resilience of the economic shocks. In this paper, the researcher investigates the different hidden economic opportunities that climate change could offer to communities to make it more resilient. The paper concludes with a recommendation about the importance of understanding the depth of climate change to low-income communities.

1. Introduction

The "Economics of Climate-Resilient Development" presents a comprehensive mitigation plan to avoid a future socio-economic crisis. The author's foresight that unless strategies are adapt effectively and efficiently today by the different communities and especially in the developing low-income countries, the world would be vulnerable to economic shocks that never been experienced before.

The book can be considered unique since it linked economic development with the techniques of adaptation. It coincides with work the reviewer published about resilience economy where approaches for enhancing people and communities are explained to reach the minimum expected adaptability and flexibility. Buheji (2018a, 2018b).

However, the work of Fankhauser and McDermott (2016) greatly focus on climate change, as the main challenge of economic development. The work will be greater if the editors ensure more inclusion and details on the nature of human being journeys.

The issue of poverty covered in the book is a good example of a foresighted socio-economic risk that needs to be mitigated to avoid deterioration due to many conditions that most would be uncontrollable due to unforeseen external factors. In earlier work, these factors were seen as the cause for more complexity of the business models, which required proactive resilient practices, Buheji (2017).

2. Resilient Development Opportunities

Choosing resilience smart alternatives that would help to reduce greenhouse gas emission and managing residual climate risks, and this is supported by a later study (Buheji, 2018a). Education, good institution and access to credit as per Fankhauser and McDermott (2016) are considered some of the resilient alternatives. However, one would debate that poverty is the biggest societal challenge of the 21st century, as many other factors compete for this causality, besides the climate challenge, such as non-communicable diseases and the rising gap between north and south. The book brings in a collection of opportunities that can be tackled in order to increase future opportunities.

3. Adaptation as a Measure of Countries Capacity

The book treats adaptation to climate change as an issue of climate-resilient development, rather than as a bespoke set of activities (flood defences, drought plans, and so on), combining climate and development challenges into a single strategy. The authors study the different vulnerabilities of developing countries to climate risks and what approaches can help to manage the disruption of the socio-economic trends. The book is well structured with concepts that can be easily followed by action plans.

The intention of coping with climate risks and locking its vulnerability helps to define future opportunities for investors. This piece of knowledge work can help investors assess climate-resilient developments in a structured and scientific way.

The editors tried to connect the paper in a way that they would holistically present economical solutions and adaptation plans for managing climate change according to the prioritized list. The lesson learned from climate-resilient cities presented in this book encourages decision-makers to develop more instruments for climate-resilient development.

4. Conclusion

The "Economics of Climate-Resilient Development" is a very important visionary book for low-income countries policymakers. The book teaches us that developments for economic resilience require us to focus on issues that would influence any progress or mitigate those issues that prevent positive outcome. Thus issues of demographic change need to be studied in developing countries in order to see how it affects its resilience capacity, i.e. in case of climate disasters. One could consider that this book is important for those who are passionate about future foresight of the socio-economic perspective which the world still need many studies to catch up with it major expected risks and turbulences, as mentioned in Buheji (2018c).

References

Buheji, M. (2018a) Role of Empathetic Engineering in Building More Resilient Green Economy. Case Study on Creating Resilient Self-Sufficient Food Security Programs in Middle East. Advances in Social Sciences Research Journal, 5(3) 148-157.

Buheji, M (2018b) Understanding the Power of Resilience Economy: An Inter-Disciplinary Perspective to Change the World Attitude to Socio-Economic Crisis, AuthorHouse, UK.

Buheji, M (2018c) Practices of Future Foresight in Management of Non-Communicable Diseases -An Early Attempt towards Focusing on 'Foresight Economy' Labs. Advances in Social Sciences Research Journal. Vol.5, No.4, pp. 344-355.

Buheji, M. (2017) Understanding Mechanisms of Resilience Economy- Live Application on a Complex Business Model. Advances in Social Sciences Research Journal, 4(14), pp. 52-64.

'CREATIVE DESTRUCTION' AND THE SHARING ECONOMY[4]

[4]Buheji, M and Ahmed, D (2017) Review Paper - Creative Destruction and the Sharing Economy, International Journal of Youth Economy, Vol 1, Issue 1, March, pp. 119-120,

Abstract

Sharing economy has developed to be more visible in many products and services around us today. The phenomena of Uber is just one example. The availability of this type of economy is very important for the development of more independent, resilient business models, today and in the future. This paper investigates the opportunities that sharing economy offers to make communities more creative, innovative and resilient.

Keywords: Sharing Economy, Creativity, Creative Destruction, Disruptive Innovation.

Introduction

As from its title, the book of 'Creative Destruction and the Sharing Economy.'

focus on the concept of 'Sharing Economy' and its role in creating creative destruction and disruptive innovation. The

Uber taxi system and its applications are discussed as 'disruptive innovation' that creates new thinking in political economy.

The book is organized around four chapters in a classic strategic way besides the introduction and the conclusion.

The book is full of repetitions and short examples from the successful Economics of Uber. However, the book more focuses on the struggle between innovation and regulation that is trying to "Destroy Uber the destroyer".

The author, Henrique Schneider, Chief Economist, Swiss Federation of SME, discusses technically how Uber economics plays as a force for economic and socio-economic development. However, the author again critiques the regulators who envisage wellbeing, but in reality, they are usually are short-sighted and can't precise expect future development. This is due that regulation is static. However, sharing economy as of Uber app is more of dynamic. The author was successful in explaining how the sharing economy is competitive and hard to expect since it is made based on interdisciplinary thinking. This interdisciplinary thinking is made in the case of Uber of law + philosophy + sociology + history, besides economics. Thus it is really an economy that is linked to different people, economy and society.

Sharing economy (i.e. doing and creating businesses from things that you don't own) managed to raise the attention of economics tools, thus leading to better market + welfare + equilibrium + profit + cost.

The author calls for a framework where the individuals are free to act and work on really as per Austria school of the economy, which combines socialist evolution with the open-ended market.

We believe that the author was successful in showing how Uber economy influenced and developed our societies and changed its behaviour to accept sharing as a concept. However, it believed that the author didn't give enough explanation how Uber economy made utility and cost to be subjective, nor did he explain how the social institution impacted the human action in this case specifically.

Opportunities Brought by Sharing Economy

The book brings in smoothly the importance of cooperative practice as an entrepreneurial opportunity. However, again, the author fails to illustrate how Uber symptom helps in "welfare promotion and maximization".

We believe the author managed to discuss how the Uber applied Austrian Economics through bringing in more volunteer groups that affected the market of a taxi. This type of pull thinking economy managed to create more realisation today about the importance of using and sharing extra access, re-defining the individual ideal inventory or capacity vs increasing the individual financial access and ownership. The case of mobility as an economy driver can be applied to any other area.

Uber economy has opened a strong positive debate how one can use societal population density, need for services sustainability, desire for community, the feel of overcoming strict government regulations, the lack of trust between sellers and buyers and sellers data to disrupt the market with the proposed business model.

The book leaves us with the wide expectation of more projects to come in relevance to Sharing Economy. The variety of disruptive innovation that used some of the sharing economies and created global companies like Pizza Hut, Amazon which uses the (1-hour sharing economy) or the Tesla Car that created even more disruption proven that such entrepreneurial driven projects can:

1 - Unlock the value of capacity
2 - Be utilise values as a Driver
3 - Use the supply side as a unique value

4 - Can utilize the customer who is in demand-side

5 - Have a business that is built on distributed market space.

Conclusion

The book is suitable as a Case Study reference book for both undergraduate and postgraduate Business, Sociology and Law Students for discussion on how Business Models are built based on Cooperation and even Collaboration. However, the reader has to be patient with high repetitions.

We believe that the book is a good reference to all entrepreneurs who are going to use the sharing economy in their business. It simulates for them how their business would influence or can influence the economy, society and technology.

Reference

Buheji, M (2016) Handbook of Inspiration Economy. Bookboon.

REVIEWING HOW 'CREATING RESILIENT ECONOMIES' CAN HELP DEVELOPING COUNTRIES IN UNCERTAIN TIMES[5]

[5]Buheji, M (2019) Reviewing How 'Creating Resilient Economies' can Help Developing Countries in Uncertain Times, American Journal of Economics, Vol. 9, Issue 5, pp. 259-263.

Abstract

This paper reviews the work of William and Vorley (2017) on the creation of more resilient economies, and then apply it to developing countries. The literature reviews, along with the synthesis of the book, help to explore the latest developments of resilience economy (RE) in relevance to the accumulated human experience and global developments in the absorbance of shocks.

The motivation of RE is measured on developing countries in general. Finally, the implications of the book for developing countries is put forward before closing on general recommendations.

Keywords: Resilience, Resilience Economy, Recovery Strategies, Developing Countries.

1.0 Introduction

This review focuses on the definitions of RE and how it evolved, especially in the last two decades. Then, RE is introduced as a discipline of requirements that have techniques, methods for each specific condition. The relation of RE on entrepreneurship, or small and medium enterprises (SMEs) are discussed, as part of the role of RE in absorbing challenges, or dealing with technological developments, or knowledge economy requirements. Buheji (2018).

After the review, the importance of the book to the developing world, especially the Arab, is discussed. This would be based on the motivation for RE and its ways of dealing with the different crisis as synthesised from the work of William and Vorley (2017) on 'resilient creation economies'. Then the author of this paper set forward the implications of this book, for all the countries with more focus on developing countries.

2.0 Literature Review

2.1 Definitions of Resilience Economy

Resilience economy is about the ability to transform and change to the circumstances without degrading the aim or the function targeted. Economic resilience is still an emerging field in the social sciences. The rationale for such work is to develop the capacity of organisations and communities' tolerance in uncertain economic times. It is a field that depends on adaptation and proactively embracing change.

Hence RE is about the prospect of bouncing back or bouncing forward. It is a field that helps the organisations, the communities of the countries to accommodate change and withstand systemic interruptions or discontinuities and to do so without disrupting the majority of the system.

2.2 Evolution of Resilience Economy as a Discipline of Requirements

Resilience has evolved from natural and physical sciences until it was adopted recently more in social sciences. This has taken many phases of transformation until it became essential to social thinking. Today RE is has become today as a proactive for how social systems are constructed and to be understood, besides how to influence any potential shocks.

Resilience Economy requires us to understand the underlying dynamics. This means we need to understand, absorb and realise: the dynamics of the economic growth, the recession and the recovery. RE focus on understanding the factors that shape and determine the nature of economic change and performance over time, instead of focusing on economic cycles only.

Buheji (2018) mentioned how RE as a concept comes from multi-disciplinary backgrounds as management, psychology, ecology, social psychology, socio-economy, sociology. Recently, RE was also joined by economic geography. RE focuses on bringing in communities from different sectors to work together to design and deliver strategic priorities and develop competitiveness.

2.3 Techniques/Methods of Resilience Economy

The techniques of resilience economy depend on monitoring systems under observation and externally induced disruption or crisis. RE try to come back to business as usual, but this not necessarily always the best solution.

Resilience has become a key concept how governments, organisations and communities should deal or prepare for external or internal shocks be it political, economic, social, technological or even legal and environmental. Also, RE helps in mitigating and eliminating the effects of such shocks or crisis.

The review of the book provides an evaluation of whether the collections of papers in this study provide academic insights. Besides the review target to investigate what implications this book carries for the future governments, organisation and communities' policies and practices.

2.4 Learning from Physiological Resiliency

The mechanics of the human body is an excellent example of resiliency. The body works on duplicating the essential components of the body to ensure there is some redundancy in the system. Buheji (2018).

Buheji (2015) on reviewing the work of Andrew Zolli and Ann Healy (2013) coincides with the work of William and Vorley on seeing that the system of the body and its cells is based on diversity where specific cells would overlap the responsibility of the other cells. The system of the body is modular, i.e. each system can almost work independently from the other. Hence, it is like a fool-proof system, or what the Japanese call poka-yoke lean system design.

The system is also adaptive and prudent (wise), besides being harmony with other basic or advanced systems. William and Vorley, illustrated this by the accident of Toyota valve factory, where the factory became on fire and made a complete halt stop to the company production of valves stopped Toyota from car productions only for five days. This was due to Re capacity that came from the strong network of Toyota with car valves suppliers, which was due to modularity and redundancy, besides adaptation in its system.

William and Vorley believe that mechanical non-disruptive systems which are based on set goals and plans to solve problems are not sufficient any more where business becoming more dynamic and work in an unstable environment. We need more biological thinking than mechanical thinking, i.e. to shape challenges, rather than to control challenges.

Instead of asking 'how good our game?' (mechanical thinking), need to think now more about 'how long our game would last, before we need to shift to another one?' (biological thinking).

3.0 Methodology

The research question of this book and literature review is 'how can the creation of more resilient economies help the developing countries in uncertain times?'.

Based on the literature they reviewed and the synthesis of the work of William and Vorley (2017), a motivation of 'how resilient economies are created'. Then, this work is reflected in how it would be created in developing countries and especially in the weakness known for these countries as the effectiveness of entrepreneurship programs and culture.

4.0 The Motivation for Creating Resilient Economies

4.1 Introduction to the Rising Importance for Creation RE

Through RE people, organisations and communities are all motivated to create resources and optimise utilising them or conserving them during times of crisis or post-crisis.

With RE, the motivation would not be for people, but in dealing with energies, social relations, knowledge, conditions and physical or natural assets.

4.2 Role of RE in Defining How to Deal with Crisis

RE focus on how we deal with the crisis. For example, riots are a social, human-induced crisis that increases conflicts and make it difficult to make proper or effective decisions in ambiguity and fussiness.

Besides the known diversity, the RE also encourage the organisations and especially the entrepreneurs to have a plan B to deal with traumas or sudden disruptions. i.e. to be both healthy and profitable, resources for this status need to be identified before and be ready for utilisation aftermath of the crisis. Buheji (2017).

RE also define other ways of dealing with the crisis to be able to bounce backwards or forward by encouraging on means that would raise the capacity to conserve on the resources utilised or considered to be essential.

The book uses experiential learning from those who managed to survive or been victimised during riots. For example, part of RE is to study how the strategies of certain small businesses helped them to survive or manage the crisis.

4.3 Role of RE on Sustaining an Effective Entrepreneurship Environment

The book focuses on the vulnerability of the entrepreneurs and small business, especially during the crisis, taking the last crisis of Greece as an example.

Studies of RE now focus on the extent of crisis and shocks on the entrepreneurs and what would differentiate their ability to resist or recover from shocks. The RE try to integrate both human capital, with innovation and entrepreneurship and creativity to enhance the readiness of the entrepreneurs. Buheji (2017).

The book shows the differentiation of knowledge economy based jobs where their ability to bounce back is better than other jobs. This raised the intersection between innovation and resilience.

5.0 Implications for Creating RE in Developing Countries

5.1 Importance of RE creation in Uncertain Time

This book is highly essential for re-evaluating the micro-economic policies in developing countries, specifically about socio-economic structures with the local entrepreneurs' empowerment policies.

Depending on positive growth, William and Vorley (2017) emphasis that the developing countries may vanish quickly when the immediate opportunities expire, or when a crisis occurs. This means more middle-class families in these developing economies could be vulnerable, and their initiatives would be less cost-effective. Smith (2013).

The book gives a direction to socio-politically congested developing countries, as in the Arab World, to re-invent its resilience by bringing the political and the business communities together. If this synergy achieved, it would bring to the communities in these developing countries to realise developments and sustain the economic growth that would lead to a differentiating resilient economy.

5.2 How RE Creation Would Enhance Developing Countries Adaptability?

One of the most chronic problems in developing countries is their rigidity in accepting change. RE as per the work of William and Vorley (2017) could ignite the capacity of the different sectors in the developing communities to remodel itself towards being more adaptable and flexible for engaging the stakeholders in its service. This very important in a current complicate delicate socio-political environment where many locations around the world and especially Arab developing countries. Since many of the developing countries trying to shift to be emerging economies, they are more competing today to attract investors and to show their resilience capability across different sectors. RE could offer this gradual convergence towards the betterment of realistic, sustainable economic performance in a short time.

5.3 Role of RE in Fostering a Realistic Innovative Environment

RE would help in fostering an economy that is based on the real innovative and entrepreneurial spirit that meet the demands for dynamic and diverse conditions. The drive to establish tolerance and resilience stimulates the competition and drive towards more innovation that creates more sustainable employment opportunities, specifically for youth in the Arab and developing countries. These attempts should lessen the impact of intrinsic and extrinsic sudden shock and reduce total socio-economic dependency on the specific type of sector or activities or resources. Buheji (2017), William and Vorley (2017).

RE is thus seen as a renewal stimulator for new paths that prevent our communities mindset from being in 'lock-in' state. This stimulation not only should encourage diversification of the products or the services, but also bring the inappropriate dynamic partnership between private, non-profit and public sectors. This would make the communities mindset shift from scarcity to an abundance of opportunities and differentiated competitiveness resources. The key performance indicators or the outcomes measures for such economies would shift towards gauging the amount of flexible and adaptable businesses created rather than several start-ups established, or amount of loans or seeds investments disbursed. Antoniades (2017).

5.4 Role of RE in Evaluating and Calibrating Developing Countries Policies

Through RE projects, the developing countries decision-maker can determine the adaptive ability of the different sectors and the different policies, including those controlled by the political economy. RE projects help to define where to invest more in relevance to the business environment, the future capital profile, including the type of human capital needed, the institutional arrangements and type of infrastructure, which are trusted criteria is highly needed post-corrupted countries. Antoniades (2017), Buheji (2017), Smith (2013).

Thus, RE can be a tool for exploiting where re-engineering or restructuring are needed most and when and for how long. Williams and Vorley (2017) of the opinion that getting involved with RE projects inspires the stakeholders to get engaged with setting a 'resilience agenda'.

5.5 RE role in Checking the Integrity of Developing Countries Labour Funds

RE found to be very important for checking the integrity of developing countries different labour funds clusters. RE would help to shift LF measures in its capacity to conceive the beneficiaries' businesses survival, or growth following a crisis, rather just disbursements of loans.

This is again very important for developing countries where many different clusters of labour funds either not effective or it is corrupted, or its return on investment could not be traced yet.

6.0 Discussion

6.1 Uniqueness of 'RE Creation' Book

William and Vorley (2017) work have much uniqueness that is not easily clear or available in other RE books. The editors used 'bottom-up approach' and in creating the common thread of the papers in the book. Therefore, RE is presented here from different backgrounds and different discipline.

The book introduces the resilience economy as a means for raising the capacity of resilience thinking and enhancing its strength as a conceptual model, through responding to external shocks and potential threats. However, the editors show how the different RE theorist and practitioners agree that there is standard rhythm about managing the capacity of the business, the community, or the country to enhance its capability to 'bouncing backwards' or 'bouncing forward'. Buheji (2019).

Besides the book bring in three types of 'recovery strategies' that represent a holistic approach to dealing with any crisis. These recovery strategies are social, economic and personal.

6.2 Implications of the book Specifically on Developing Countries

The book focuses on how people, organisations, governments and communities could impact the economy and make it more resilient.

The book shows that RE could have its influence on many sectors, despite being focused on the public sector. The book set a clear direction for establishing both cultural and social base for the best conditions that enhance the adaptability, the responsiveness and the flexibility to the different potential types of crises. This is highly important for resilience economy audit that would be highly beneficial for developing countries.

The book is very suitable for think-tanks to the world leaders, but specifically again complicated economies as the developing countries. It is a piece of reference that is even suitable for policymakers and academics of multi-disciplines.

6.3 RE Creation and Communities Mindset Change

Despite that the editors William and Vorley (2017) confirm that there are 'no one size fits all' RE programs and that each program need a particular measurement or be approached based on the conditions of the targeted beneficiary, or on the context which they are applied in, the book carries many holistic approach that is suitable for serious countries that want to change. Besides, the book encourages static countries as in the developing Arab countries to adopt resilient solutions based on the external challenges which come through experimentation only. Antoniades (2017).

7.0 Recommendations & Conclusion

Creation of economic resilience is not any more a crisis management program, but in a future growth and development path framework that is related to the capacity and the well to survive and differentiate.

This theoretical analysis of resilience creation foster resilience thinking and the opportunities it carries to re-frame and reform any economy and especially the economies of the developing countries. The comprehensive approaches offered in the work of William and Vorley (2017) is highly suitable for further research and development for many different sectors not mentioned in the book and provides an excellent base for cultures and communities that have the clear intent to improve its adaptability and responsiveness to external or internal challenges.

Academics and practitioners could benefit from this reviewed book as it would help to bring their collective efforts and could create a common language for those that need to respond to the crisis more effectively.

References

Antoniades, A (2017) The New Resilience of Emerging and Developing Countries: Systemic Interlocking, Currency Swaps and Geoeconomics, Global Policy, 8(2), pp. 170-180.

Buheji, M (2019) Theories of Organisational Resilience. A book Review. International Journal of Inspiration & Resilience Economy, 3(1): 33-33.

Buheji, M (2018) Understanding the Power of Resilience Economy: An Inter-Disciplinary Perspective to Change the World Attitude to Socio-Economic Crisis, AuthorHouse, UK.

Buheji, M. (2017) Understanding Mechanisms of Resilience Economy- Live Application on a Complex Business Model. Advances in Social Sciences Research Journal, 4(14), pp. 52-64.

Buheji, M (2015) Book Review 'Resilience' for Andrew Zolli and Ann Healy, Journal of Inspiration Economy, Vol 2, Issue.1, (March)

Smith, E (2013) Strengthening Resilience in Developing Countries, the globalist, https://www.theglobalist.com/strengthening-resilience-in-developing-countries/ Accessed: 1/6/2019

William, N and Vorley, T (2017) Creating Resilient Economies - Entrepreneurship, Growth and Development in Uncertain Times, E-Elgar.

PART TWO

APPROACHES TOWARDS RESILIENT COMMUNITIES

UNDERSTANDING MECHANISMS OF RESILIENCE ECONOMY

- *Live Application on a Complex Business Model*[6]

[6] Buheji, M. (2017) Understanding Mechanisms of Resilience Economy- Live Application on a Complex Business Model. Advances in Social Sciences Research Journal, 4(14), p. 52-64.

Abstract

"Resilience" as a concept has been re-discovered by many researchers from different disciplines in the last few years as it answers the demands for sustainable dynamical systems and way thinking that need to be addressed to rehabilitate different problems in our world today.

This paper reviews the concept of resilience in order to develop from it a proposed mechanism for tackling problems and techniques that would lead to the inspiration of the business model of any organization or society. An application of the proposed mechanism is implemented on the Water Supply Service loss and leakages as a challenging problem that is faced usually by most of the water utility and authority companies all over the world, but with varying magnitude, is reviewed. Being a complex business model, going through different challenges in many developed and developing countries, resilience mechanism is applied to identify how to improve the capacity of the system and make it more resilient without increasing its expenditure or affecting it supply stability.

The study goes to see how the mechanism of resilience economy, adopted from the literature reviewed, could help to contribute to our understanding of the evolution of such system mechanism if we really to adopt a resilient mindset.

Keyword:

Resilience, Resilience Economy, Coexistence, Intolerance, Inspiration Economy

1.0 Introduction

The concept of 'resilience' was first adopted within systems ecology in the 1970s, where it ignited the research of the cybernetics along with the complex systems theory.

Resilience today became an operational strategy and part of many risk and development management programs.

Resilience Economy (RE) is a new concept and field that is still in its early exploration and its focus on balancing the welfare impact, whether in time of peace and disaster. Therefore, RE does not only depend on the physical characteristics of the event or its direct impacts in terms of lost lives and assets. (Duval and Vogel, 2008; Rose, 2004).

Resilience economy mechanisms targets to establish welfare impacts in the business model, which depend on the ability of the economy to cope, recover, and reconstruct and therefore, to minimize consumption losses. This ability that RE builds in the business models can be referred to as the microeconomic resilience. (Duval and Vogel, 2008).

In this study, we would try to understand from the literature review the influence that the mechanisms of resilience economy can bring in the different business models and especially in complex one, and then we explore how this has been used during inspiration labs that brought major improvement to the preservation and conservation of a country essential natural resources, that water. (Fernandez, 2006).

The paper discusses the economic resilience from different relevant points as culture and environment and what learnings can be taken relevant to 'stability'. Particular resilience practices are focused on as resilience in decision making, material diversity, investigations resilience, social integration and resilience towards sustainability in natural resources which is the focus of the context of the study.

2.0 Literature Review

2.1 Definition of Resilience

"Resilience" is about the ability to absorb shocks while continuing to function. It's a word that has gained a lot of currency in recent years as more and more people realize that we have some big shocks headed our way: financial shocks, energy shocks, environmental shocks, as we as social unrest and international conflict. Rose (2004).

So resilience focus on the mental and then physical ability to recover quickly from depression, illness or misfortune. The physical property of the material that can resume its shape after being stretched or deformed; elasticity. The positive ability of a system or company to adapt itself to the consequences of a catastrophic failure caused by the power outage, a fire, a bomb or similar (particularly

IT systems, archives). While the word resilient means can endure, be bendable, be flexible, be strong without cracking, or with high ability to manage the impact of tribulation.

Resilience means we would be more ready to act as humans where mistakes are prone; however, management of mistakes is what we should be ready for.

2.2 Resilience & Persistence

Resilience needs persistence which is a continuance course of action despite difficulty or opposition. As with persistence, we build the ability to recover from misfortune or change.

Perrings, C. (1998) Collaborative work between ecologists and economists has used the ecological concept of resilience to explore the relative persistence of different states of nature. The concept of resilience has two main variants. One is concerned with the time taken for a disturbed system to return to some initial state and is due to Pimm (1984). A second is concerned with the magnitude of disturbance that can be absorbed before a system flips from one state to another and is due to Holling (1986).

2.3 Understanding Resilience from Nature

The ecological concept of resilience focus on change in economy-environment systems. The linkages between resilience and the stability of dynamical systems as biodiversity and the sustainability of alternative states. Walker and Cooper (2011).

Recent developments in modelling the resilience of joint economy-environment systems suggest the advantages of analysing the change in the system as a Markov process, the transition probabilities between states offering a natural measure of the resilience of the system in such states. It is argued that this 'emergent property' of the collaboration between ecology and economics has far-reaching implications for the way we think about, model and manage the environmental sustainability of economic development. (Duval and Vogel, 2008).

2.4 Resilience & Adaptation

Resilience reflects a general consensus about the necessity of adaptation through an endogenous crisis (Wong-Parodi et al., 2015). The generalization of complex systems theory as a methodology of power has ambivalent sources. While the redefinition of the concept can be directly traced to the work of the ecologist Crawford S. Holling (1986), the deployment of complex systems theory is perfectly in accord with the later philosophy of the Austrian neoliberal Friedrich Hayek.

Since resilience deals with aspects of stability and adaptation, it offers then system equilibria, thus offering alternative measures in relevance to enhancing the capacity of a system to retain productivity following disturbance. This support the inspiration economy main requirement, i.e. the ability to shift towards capacity vs demand. Levin et al. (1998). Therefore, resilience became an enabler for managing the diversity in the Work Place and in managing the endogenous integration within the society.

2.5 Resilience in Business Models

Birchall (2009) focused on the importance of resilience designs in the business models to minimise economic crisis and improve the positive impact; using cooperative enterprises as a reference. Birchall showed how the consumer, worker and financial cooperative models all remained financially sound; reporting an increased turnover and growth despite the high economic instability. (Nsouli, 1995).

Birchall showed how the cooperative model of enterprise not only survives the crisis, but also able to withstand crisis, maintaining the livelihoods of the communities in which they operate.

Therefore, establishing resilience in business models can contribute to the organisation's inspiration and effectiveness since it raises its ability to undermined changes in the internal and external environment in a very efficient way as mentioned by Sosna et al. (2010).

Sosna and his team showed that resilience mechanisms built-in business models of Spanish dietary products that were threatened by economic recession and heightened competition lead to help the business flourish and survive more and more. Resilience in the model of the dietary organisation made it outperform its competitors by a wide margin.

Resilience in the business model means that we build a model that would meet high challenges and different life problems. It is a model that needs positive behaviour in meeting challenges which leads to increasing the capacity to demands. The role of the model is also a source of inspiration and directly or indirectly improve the overall socio-economic development. The model should help to ignite sustained feeling inspiration where it can be a point of reference for resilience economy, as shown in Figure (1).

Figure (1) Components of a Resilience
Economy Business Model

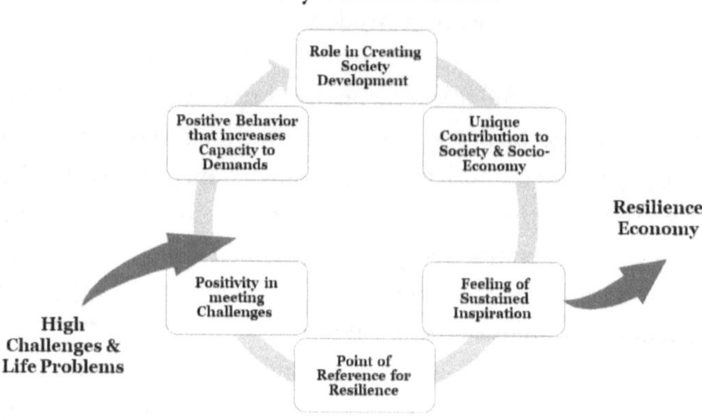

2.6 Demand for Resilience Mechanisms in Our Societies

Resilience mechanisms are rarely discussed in the literature, even though it is highly demanded all types of sectors and business in our societies and communities. Whatever the social status, the level of civilization and type of social fabric, resilience mechanisms can play a great role in creating better outcome with minimal resources.

Resilience in the designs of business models is highly needed today for the mindset of the middle class and decision-makers in our societies, or those individuals responsible for the community services and development.

Many factors influence the identification of the type of resilience needed in the business model; one of these factors is the problem that triggers the need for establishing a resilient mechanism. Therefore, we need to determine the particular behaviour of resilience that can be used to deal with the social problem.

2.7 Introduction Resilience Economy

Resilience economy is spreading more and more indifferent disciplines research such as in politics, economics, technology, finance, urban and environmental issues, security, social problems, psychology, problem-solving, legal issues and policy management. (Kumpfer, 1999)

Resilience Economy requires identifying the scope of the business model in relevance to its socio-economic role, through recognizing or analysing the model problem or challenges.

Resilience economy is much related to inspiration economy, as mentioned in the work of Buheji (2016). Resilience economy requires restoration and adaptation while inspiration economy focuses on adoption and innovative development with minimal resource. Please refer to Figure (2)

Figure (2) Relation of Resilience Economy
and Inspiration Economy.

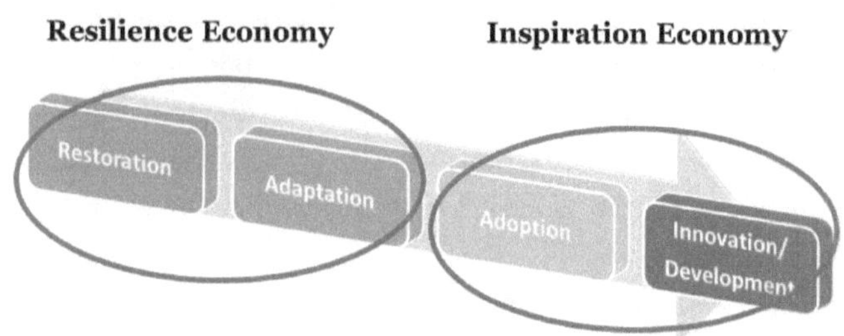

Resilience economy focuses on managing the deviations in the socio-economic mechanisms. Non-Resilience is considered a weakness is considered a weakness in the business model, and it is an abnormal state because it does not reflect the social aspect of humanity.

Resilience Economy focuses on studying the business model that lead to the current living conditions of poor immigrants. For example, we need more resilience practices from Europeans, who are accepting African and Asian migrants every day in their countries and where those migrants are settling in urban cities that are known for their social mobility. We need resilience practices in dealing with people from the underdeveloped areas of the Slums, where deep poverty, crime, delinquency, rift families and ethnic strife are preventing youth from seeing their dreams possible or achievable.

Same applies in the issue of dealing with the business model that guarantees the sustainability of essential water and energy supply. The business model needs to be resilient enough to minimize energy or water loss, while maintaining continuity of services.

Resilience economy, therefore, aims to study the deviant behaviour and identify the social problem and then find means to solutions that would help develop the socio-economic status.

2.8 Business Model Resilience & Deviant Behaviour

When individuals realize the existence of a business model problem they are working on, they take different and varied positions towards this. The positions of each individual differ according to the degree of proximity or distance from the problem. Their ability shift to focus on distancing themselves from the problem; instead of deeply understanding the opportunities of resilience in the model itself. (World Bank, 2013).

Since resilience is about mitigation and management of feelings or practices that lead to the indifference, people need to control their attitudes and practices in a way that would enhance the business model resilience.

In almost every type of speciality when the industrialization and urbanization increase the socio-economic problems increases in a very disorganized and deviant way that affects human behaviour and the way, the business model is delivered. This applies even to water utility services which are the context of this paper.

The resilience mechanism helps to build socio-economic disintegration in the business model between the concerned parties, thus establishing Total People Involvement that would undergo with the value system in the community targeted.

Resilience is considered a compact against any socio-economic disintegration that leads to more dependence on specific resources in the business model. Resilient models do not mean conforming to the standards and values of the community, but it is about the ability to adapt. For example, building resilience economy model to manage the issue of migration from south to north would need more resilience in the education of immigrants to solve their problems by creating for them mindsets that would build self-fulfilment supported by mentorship and educational programs.

The concept of perverse behaviour refers to the deviation from causes of consistent behaviour. The behaviour of an incompatible business model usually creates a challenge to the legitimacy of social norms. Through resilience, we can overcome the uncoordinated business processes efforts, which lead to behaviourally deviant practices.

Resilient models prevent the interference between socio-economic problems, deviation and disintegration. With resilient models, all sources of frustrations would be dealt with as early as possible to avoid reaching disintegration breaks out.

2.9 From Unstable Socio-Economy Practices to Resilience Economy Mechanisms

Today more than ever before we need resilience mechanism to make our communities readier to be challenged as opposed to what might be learned from interaction and from challenging the current state of our lives.

Resilience economy mechanisms focus on the classification of the business model problems that an organisation or a community faces towards the pattern of stability adaptation.

In order to shift from unstable socio-economy to a resilient economy, we need first to deal with the set of recurrent problems resulting from adapting to the external environment. To direct the outcome of the set of problems to satisfy the different business model component needs.

In order also to shift from unstable socio-economy, we need to build mechanisms that turn the negative effect of the problems to a positive one. This would eliminate gradually the negative behaviour that demands confrontation and increase the probabilities for achieving the model stability, as illustrated in Figure (3).

Figure (3) Shifting from Unstable to Resilience Economy

In order to build resilience in the business model people need to be more aware of the problem, the clearer the problem becomes the more we can create a transformation from unstable socio-economy to a resilience economy. The resilience mechanisms should help overcome problems and overcome the possibility of any mental rejection.

Therefore business models problems can be classified into fundamental business model problems linked to the lack of basic failure to deliver services or products relevant to the core of the business model, or non-satisfactory business model problems, or synergetic business model problem that is linked to the bad relations between different stakeholders of business model or the problem.

2.10 Role of Resilience Economy in Managing Complex Models

The resilience practices help to mitigate the level of problems in the business model. Hence with resilience mechanisms, we mitigate the strong impact of problems on the surrounding socio-economic conditions, or minimize the adverse conditions and results that are mainly caused by socio-economic problem affects, or reduce the harmful conditions which are directly or indirectly the product of the socio-economic problems on the business model.

Resilience economy mechanisms help to manage the challenges caused by the vulnerability of problem failures and raise the targeted business model adaptive capacity, as Figure (4) shows. The larger the population density that the business model applies for, the more complex the problem becomes and the more diverse its causes and sources, and the more its forms and types. Röhn et al. (2015).

Figure (4) Role of Resilience in Managing Challenges

With the spirit persistence and the mechanisms of resilience, the creation of successful business models even in a complex environment is highly possible as this leads to the greater insight that, in turn, leads to new waves of seeing hidden opportunities (Buheji, 2016). Once this resilience is established in the targeted culture, the inspiration starts to enhance our abilities to see solutions inside each difficulty, thus helping us to focus on sustained resilient models' outcomes.

Creating inspired resilience economy business models need to maintain the diversity of solutions with high levels of communication. This establishes resilient business models that can apply the formula for the sustenance of change. As we go through the complex business model, we need to go through four stages, as shown in Figure (5). The first stage concerns going through a shift in cultural focus from 'what is wrong' to 'what works' in the business model. This means we need to be more resilient in terms of observing and discovering. Once we can absorb, opportunities of resilience better outcomes can be generated.

Figure (5) Journey of Resilience in the Inspiration Labs

2.11 Development of Resilience Economy Mindset through Inspiration Engineering

Studies show that the business model is healthy (with high communication) and is profitable (with high value-added) practices. The healthier and more profitable the business model is the more its mechanisms would be resilient. The stability that will lead to acceptance; this establishes the first cycle in learning resilience. As we move towards greater sustainability, we will feel the importance of abundance thinking.

Resilient mindsets will develop individuals and communities that are cooperative and self-sufficient, self-initiated and proactive

(Birchall, 2009). Moreover, resilient mindsets lead to more positive thinking, making it more likely to be risk-takers with a high ability to manage uncertainties. This is shown in Figure (6).

Figure (6) Characteristics of a Resilient Mindset

Therefore, it could be said that resilience mechanism creates an inspirational edge in the business model. Once the resilience of the model is started, change agents are needed. Through the spirit of resilience, we can establish research and development clusters within the organisation.

We can deliver more focused goodwill working practices that are reflected in the socio-economic business model outcome.

At we start the process of observations and exploring opportunities in the business model, the capacity for resilience automatically raised. Our ability to absorb what we learned during the exploration stages will increase our ability to find more opportunities, thus enhancing our knowledge and inspiration sources. (Buheji, 2006).

As we synthesise and absorb the results of observation, we start to shift towards a new realisation of 'what we can do' to change and develop our mindsets about the business model, as illustrated in Figure (7).

Figure (7) Capacity for Business Model Resilience during after the Inspiration Lab and its Role in Changing Mindsets

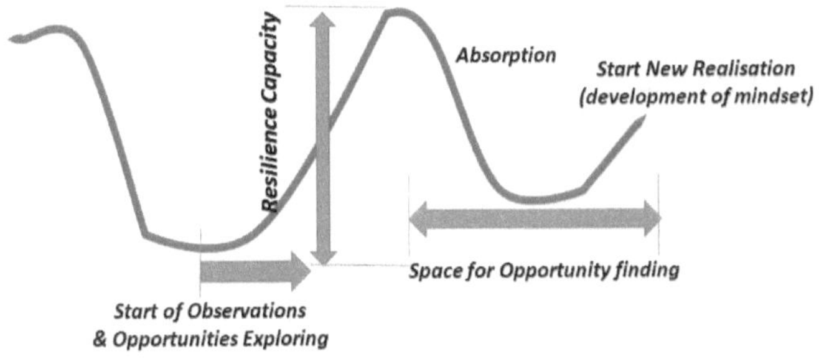

Reivich and Shatte (2003), authors of 'Resilience Factor', found that overcoming life's hurdles requires us to break down a problem into parts and determine which one can be solved first; we then fix what we can and then let the rest go. Resilience in Inspiration Labs is developed gradually based on this practice. Through practising more and more, the capturing of opportunities, understanding the challenges, and working on the development of a model, we can clearly reflect and learn from the inspiration journey.

With the presence of resilience absorption techniques, the amplification of the problem is in control. Thus, we avoid reaching a situation where the general public works on their discontent and discomfort. With resilience economy, we can mitigate the possibility of amplification of the problem and minimize its size and effects in a way that it can be easily handled by the reformers.

3.0 Methodology

The research methodology employed in this paper is a qualitative case study. The case study was chosen as a method because it is suitable for situations that include complex and multiple variables and processes (Yin, 2003). A longitudinal case study that was carried over a period of 6 months examined the complex business model of water production management in the kingdom of Bahrain. With this kind of qualitative method, it was important to capture the resilience mechanisms used during the inspiration lab that lead to creating a resilience economy compliant business model is relevant to water production with minimal water loss.

The case study enabled an investigation into real-life events about specific evidence of resilience practices that started with interviews and observations. The paper attempts to address the research question: "How can Resilience Economy Mechanisms work to inspire complex Business Models?', i.e. ensuring the transformation of the model to be more robust and agile.

As is typical in case studies (Meredith, 1998), the case data were collected from multiple sources: thematic discussions, workshops and interviews with water authority representatives, besides concerned stakeholders. Following the principles of action research, the researcher and the actors in the case wanted to solve the urgent, immediate problem of the business model and this reflected on the development of the process of problem-solving and great experiential learning teamwork.

The interviews and trial and error field testing under what is called inspiration labs helped to get the water authority decision-makers and key stakeholders more attached to the development of a better business model that handles water loss in a country that is surrounded by sea and with no sweat water except the little remaining wells.

The business model of water production and supply directorate was based on the supply of pure water from main stations to every consumer in the most efficient way, i.e. with minimal loss. Through Inspiration Engineering and Labs and unique approaches in problem solving resilient business model was pushed with the purpose to minimise the water loss even with the fast expansion of the water network system, due to boom in population.

In this case, the socio-economic issue was minimising loss of the 40% leakage in the utility water supply network by inspiring the water authority as an organisation, and enhancing its team's ability to discover early underground leakages and losses through observation and forecasting, and then by applying a level of intelligent decision making. The techniques went through the following main steps in order to gradually enhance the mechanisms of economic resilience in the water authority business model:

Step (1) Understanding the Problem to be Solved

We can't start any problem solving without understanding what is the essence of the problem, i.e. realising the amount of water loss in the country because of system leakage between the source (the main water desalination stations) and delivery points (customers' water input points); despite the increase in the maintenance budget for water pipes and the overall water network.

Step (2): Realising the impact of the problem on natural resources in the future.

We started here by understanding the taxonomy of 'water loss' and its differentiation from 'water leakage', then applying this differentiation to check the difference.

Step (3): Outline the Scientific Method for Problem Solving

In order to outline the problem, we needed to start setting proper resilience analysis of the business model and how the water authority handles the water leakage incidents and accidents by asking the participating teams to:

a) Codify the type of water loss and leakage.
b) Classify the categories of water loss and leakage in terms of place, time, type of area, pipe designs and detection equipment.
c) Specifying the relation and the correlation between seen (visible) and hidden (invisible) water loss (both from an analysis of previous history and field observations).

Step (4): Studying Attitudes in terms of Inspiration Economy Requirements

Without understanding the attitudes towards the business model problem can't be solved; thus, in this stage, we need to start:

- Identify the types of emergency readiness relevant to stopping water loss (both the seen and the hidden).
- Identify the average length of time taken to rectify a loss of water by type and area, besides the type of field response team needed.
- Understand all the challenges in compacting water loss and leakage as regards the type and amount of consumer areas, the age of the water network, the level of consumption, the type of real estate (i.e. normal domestic consumer, public consumer or a private company, etc.).

Step (5): Start Reasoning with regard to the Problem to ease the Complexity of the Water Supply Business Model (by Applying Suitable Convergent and Divergent Thinking Approaches).

Using both convergent and divergent thinking is very important for creating an opportunity from a challenge or a problem. In order to achieve this, we need to:

- Start reasoning the type and amount of water leakage by the level of building heights and the size of the population.
- Use reasoning to re-engineer the process of water loss and water leakage, and the way this impact the response team readiness. This should help to identify and then remove the non-value-added steps.
- Train, drill and deploy teams to effectively isolate the area network from the main water supply network.
- Enhance water loss detection equipment in areas that are prone to experience hidden water loss due to their history, type of design, and forecast data.
- Start piloting projects in three main areas/types of water consumer: old areas, new areas, large consumers.

Part (6): Start Re-phrasing the Problem

In order to solve a complex problem, we need to re-phrase it, by:

- Categorise the type of challenges in each area and segregate the issues of illegal connections that count for part of the water loss problem.
- Design specific water pipes for tight areas which would be unique in size and thickness; these include characteristics to make them flexible yet robust.

Part (6): Reducing the Problem's Complexity

Both the business model and the problem complexity were reduced throughout the inspiration lab journey in order to create a more resilient economy model through:

- Understanding the types of defect in water meters that lead to slow detection and hence slow response of the emergency team.
- Understanding the places where leakage occurs inside houses and study trends or repetitions in terms of the types of connection.
- Building a 'Water Loss Intelligence Programme' that will enhance (i.e. inspire) the Water Authority to respond proactively to potential water loss on time and with high availability, better efficiency, and more effectively.
- Applying a 'Mitigation of Risks Programme' to support the 'Water Loss Intelligence Programme'.

This project helped to reduce the business model complexity and make it more resilient and also reduced the country water loss by 30%. The details of the numbers of all the above were removed to maintain confidentiality.

4.0 Discussion & Conclusion

Working on applying Resilience Economy mechanisms on critical national issues as major water loss could be a very strong technique to handle complex business models of different nature. With resilience mechanisms focused on business models development and problem-solving, we can improve the welfare impacts on many types of socio-economic issues. With macro-economic resilience, we can manage the distribution of losses or mitigate the causes of vulnerability. When our systems are economically resilient, we would be more ready to mitigate risks and absorb shocks.

In a resilient economy, improved business models can influence positively more the socio-economy and enhance the learning outcome. The learnings from the water authority loss and leakage case study are that business models can be far more resilient if we focus on its socio-economic system and work on to compensate its immediate losses, however complex it is. Therefore, it is advised that more research work is done to freely generalise the importance of resilient economy mechanisms and its ability to minimize welfare losses for any type of business model regardless of its given magnitude.

Reference

Birchall, J (2009) Resilience of the Cooperative Business Model in Times of Crisis, International Labour Organisation http://www.ilo.org/empent/Publications/WCMS_108416/lang--en/index.htm

Buheji, M (2016) Handbook of Inspiration Economy. Bookboon. ISBN: 978-87-403-1318-5. http://bookboon.com/en/handbook-of-inspiration-economy-ebook

Duval, R. and L. Vogel, (2008) Economic resilience to shocks. The role of structural policies, OECD

Fernandez, R (2016) 5 Ways to Boost Your Resilience at Work, Harvard Business Review, June.

Hill, E; Wial, H and Wolman, H (2008) Exploring Regional Economic Resilience, Working Paper, Institute of Urban and Regional Development. https://www.econstor.eu/handle/10419/59420

Holling CS (1986) Resilience and stability of ecological systems. Annual Review of Ecology and Systematics 4: 1–23.

Holling CS (1986) Resilience of ecosystems: Local surprise and global change. In: Clark WC, Munn RE (eds) Sustainable Development of the Biosphere: Cambridge: Cambridge University Press, 292–317.

Kumpfer, K (1999) The Resilience Framework, Factors and Processes Contributing to Resilience, Resilience and Development. Part of the series Longitudinal Research in the Social and Behavioral Sciences: An Interdisciplinary Series, pp 179-224.

Lange O (1949) The practice of economic planning and the optimum allocation of resources. Econometrica 17: 166–171.

Nsouli SM, (eds) (1995) Resilience and growth through sustained adjustment: The Moroccan experience. International Monetary Fund Occasional Paper No. 117. Washington, DC: International Monetary Fund.

Perrings, C. (1998) Resilience in the Dynamics of Economy-Environment Systems, Environmental Resource Economical, Vol. 11 (3-4): pp. 503-520.

Reivich, K and Shattle, A (2003) The Resilience Factor: 7 Keys to Finding Your Inner Strength and Overcoming Life's Hurdles, Harmony; Reprint edition (October 14, 2003)

Röhn, O., A. Caldera Sánchez, M. Hermansen and M. Rasmussen, (2015) Economic resilience: A new set of vulnerability indicators for OECD countries, OECD Economics Department Working Papers, No. 1249, OECD Publishing, Paris.

Rose, A (2004) Defining and measuring economic resilience to disasters, Disaster Prevention and Management: An International Journal, Vol. 13 Issue: 4, pp.307-314, https://doi.org/10.1108/09653560410556528

Sondermann, D (2016) Towards more resilient economies: the role of well-functioning economic structures, Reports No. 1984 November, European Central Bank, Working Paper.

Sosna, M; Nelly, R; Rodriguez, T; Velamuri, S (2010) Business Model Innovation through Trial-and-Error Learning: The Naturhouse Case, Long Range Planning, Volume 43, Issues 2–3, April–June 2010, Pages 383-407

Walker, J and Cooper, M (2011) Genealogies of Resilience, Washington, DC: World Bank.

Wong-Parodi, G; Fischhoff, B; Strauss, B (2015) Resilience vs. Adaptation: Framing and action, Climate Risk Management 10: 1–7.

World Bank (2013) World Development Report 2014: Risk and Opportunity—Managing Risk for Development,

Yin, R. (2003) Case Study Research, Third Edition Sage

FRAMEWORK FOR MITIGATING COMING SOCIOECONOMIC CRISIS[7]

[7]Buheji, M and Ahmed, D (2019) Framework for Mitigating Coming (Foresight) Socioeconomic Crisis, American Journal of Economics; 9(6): pp. 320-327.

Abstract

In the last decade, the economic crisis has been in rapid rhythm spikes, with a frequency never like before. The future foresight even found to carry more sudden and unpredictable spikes for both the economy and the socio-economy. Such foresight of socio-economic crisis unless mitigated it would cause catastrophic deterioration to the quality of life, where areas of education, health and stability would be negatively affected.

The objective of the paper is to investigate the types of socio-economic crisis that can be foresighted. The researchers try to approach this through qualitatively monitoring the developments of the socio-economic models and define specific areas of how to turn 'challenges into opportunities. The framework proposed in this paper target to bring-in sustained outcomes that can change how we deal with the coming socio-economic challenges. The conclusion has clear implications on the way many communities and countries are addressing sustainable development goals (SGDs).

Keywords: Socio-economic Crisis, Future Foresight, Socio-economic foresight, Resilience Economy, Inspiration Labs, SDGs, Mitigating Socioeconomic Crisis.

1.0 Introduction

Most emerging economies are trying to differentiate their growth and development by differentiating their socio-economic vulnerability to external and internal factors. Thus, the world is expected to experience a transformation from the traditional 'hard economic interventions' to more 'foresighted socio-economic interventions' that focuses on the integration of multi-disciplinary approaches towards a specific country or community problem, or development needs. Graham (2019).

This paper discusses the types of the coming and the foresighted socio-economics crisis and risks, with a focus on the contemporary ones. The literature of the impact of socio-economic challenges on the quality of life is reviewed, considering their linkages to sustainable development goals (SDGs). Astrov et al. (2018).

The researchers review the possible wealth that can be generated through managing the foresighted socio-economic issues, or re-inventing then which would lead to raising the targeted community socio-economic preparedness through focusing on the 'availability'. Then, proactive preparations for the socio-economic crisis are proposed with the suggestion to be linked with the foresighted national plans. Buheji (2019a).

This longitudinal study is part of the International Inspiration Economy Project (IIEP), which uses a methodology called Inspiration Labs (ILs) to solve the current or the foresighted socio-economic through focusing on models that can be generalised, Buheji (2019c). All the ILs were conducted by the researchers directly through the period from 2015 till 2019. The ways that socio-economic models are built to engage the middle class in their socio-economic challenges and make them active in identifying coming challenges. Buheji (2019a).

The reviewed literature helps to develop the methodology that lead to categorising the socio-economic crisis preventions by mainly two types: prevention of crisis (called for short PC) and mitigation of crisis (called for short MC). Such categorisation can suggest further research about the role of the community and their type of economic empowerment if they are to absorb socio-economic crisis in the future.

2.0 Literature Review

2.1 Types of Socio-Economics Risks

Systematic examination of socio-economic information helps to identify potential threats, risks, emerging issues and opportunities. For example, any negative impacts on human welfare such as the provision of essential services of (food, water, energy, transport, communications, etc.) would help to improve the psychological impacts. i.e. Mitigation of such risks would improve the confidence and the trust in socio-economy. Astrov et al. (2018).

Through conducting risks evaluation of the socio-economic challenge and then comparing the results with best sustainability criteria, we can determine the magnitude of tolerance that would improve the social values.

Structural shifts in global geopolitical, economic, social, technological and environmental conditions, all have led to drastic consequences on many countries socio-economic portfolios.

OECD itself has published an analysis of the nature of current and likely future global shocks and the associated risk drivers, concluding that the likelihood of such shocks being experienced. The key drivers of socio-economic risks and impacts are as likely to be the unexpected interaction analysed as a complex adaptive system, and that needs to be cross-boundary, and cross-disciplinary.

Since 2013 the world has been witnessing slow socio-economic growth in almost all regions of the world. While the world economy was expected to grow by 3.9% in 2018 and 2019, the trade tensions between the US and China and the human-made disasters and was has reduced this expectation. The migration from and to countries such as the situation in Argentina and Turkey, and the turmoil in many auto industries in India and Germany, besides the tightening of the economic development in China, are creating the even deeper socio-economic crisis.

The tightening of the economic situation is causing more weakening of many non-resilient fragile communities. This can be seen clearly in the serious challenges which many countries, with considerable uncertainty about their capacity to manage their future foresight.

2.2 Contemporary Socio-economic Crisis

Many world experts have been warning about the economic crisis coming in 2020, but the literature is scarce about the coming socio-economic crisis in the years to come, despite the technological and general materialistic quality of life achievements.

In 2009, Greece suffered a wide-range of socioeconomic challenges that led to sharp rise in unemployment rates, precarious work regimes, rapid increases in poverty level, dramatic increases in the number of uninsured citizens, substantial income loss, widened income inequality, exacerbation of the demographic problem, disruption of social cohesion, political instability, and migration and refugee issues. Stylianidis and Souliotis (2019).

In particular, unemployment rates rocketed in Greece from 7.8% in 2008 to 24.9% in 2015 and 23.1% in December 2016 (Eurostat,2017). The Greek poverty community rose from 28.1% in 2008 to 36% in 2014 and 35.7% in 2015. The Greek, middle class lost up to 70% of their household income (Hellenic Statistical Authority, 2015).

Since 2009, the Greece socio-economic incident has been repeated in different countries as in Venezuela and many countries in Africa. However, if you observe that common thread of these contemporary socio-economic crises is the amount of increasing income inequality in favour of the high-income population. In certain countries, and due to human-made disasters and wars, this is causing continuous unsettlement and migration. This is precisely what is happening to the Syrians, the Iraqi's, the Afghani's and this are one of the causes for the increase of the inequalities within the developing countries in per capita GDP. Stylianidis and Souliotis (2019).

The other issue of socio-economic challenges is the decline in mobility in advanced economies. This caused the most disadvantaged and the marginalised people to get very low paid jobs that led to the decline in community dynamics. In the means while in developing countries as in the Arab world, the number of those living in relative poverty has risen even significantly. The latest war in the Arab world even increased the incidence of poverty diseases and malnutrition, especially in countries such as Syria and Yemen.

2.3 Understanding the Essence of Socio-Economic Future Foresight

2.3.1 Importance of Future Foresight to Our Socio-economies

Foresight is a future intelligence-gathering that is systematic, participatory, and medium-to-long-term vision-building process aimed at present-day decisions and mobilising joint actions.

Socio-economic foresight is based on sensitive research that uses quantitative and/or qualitative methods oriented towards the future at the junction of dream and reality aimed at shaping a more sustainable world.

Qualitative socio-economic foresight is useful for the elaboration of long-term visions having a broad socio-economic scope such as medium- to long-term policy strategies. Buheji (2019a).

2.3.2 Importance of Socio-Economic Crisis Foresight to SDGs

The UN Sustainable Development Goals (SDGs) have listed 17 sustainable development goals (SDGs) to transform our world by 2030. There are 8 direct socio-economic goals among these 17 goals which are: SDG1 and SDG2 which focus on zero poverty and zero hunger, then the SDG3 which focus on good health and wellbeing, followed by SDG4 which targets quality of education, then SDG5 which about gender equality, followed by SDG6 and SDG7 which are both about clean water, sanitation and affordable clean energy. Then last important goal among the top eight is the SDG8 which focus on decent work while maintaining economic growth. Graham (2019).

The rest of the SDGs, SDG9 till SDG 17 also has an indirect influence on the socio-economic stability, growth and development. i.e. the slow capacity to innovate or reduced inequality would definitely affect the socio-economic stability. Same applies for environmental issues.

Hence, synchronising projects with UN-SDGs would help to eliminate the significant socio-economic crisis that usually is triggered by these sources. The SDGs serve as a source for a paradigm shift from traditional development assistance to a transformative agenda with actions driven as much at the local, national and regional level. Graham (2019).

Focusing on the SDGs integration helps to align the socio-economic development with international efforts to find practical solutions to emerging global issues and development challenges.

Despite the world have done great achievement in reducing the extreme poverty rates and managed to bring it down by half, since 1990; still one in five people in developing region lives on less than $ 1.25 a day. Millions more are making little more, while many are at risk of falling back into poverty. The problem is that many countries still with poverty as the lack of income and resources, instead of more issues that bring sustainable development of the livelihood. If the SDGs are going to be addressed well in any country, issues as social discrimination, or exclusion from society, and non-participation in decision-making need to be well exploited. This what would eliminate risks to the minimum and at the same time, ensure consistent approaches towards the claimed SDGs.

32.3.3 Impact of Socio-Economic Foresight on the Quality of Life

Stylianidis and Souliotis (2019) found that the impact of repeated socio-economic crisis could trigger up to 35% increase in suicide rates due to the potential increase in unemployment that leads to financial hardship. For example, the latest socioeconomic crisis in Greek has led to incurred adverse effects on the health of the Greek population and has produced significant mental distress.

Studies show now that decrease in socio-economic security has negative influences. For example, instable socio-economic conditions have made youth delay marriage decisions and that reduced fertility rates and led to an increase also in divorce rates which caused further economic crises. Buheji (2018a).

2.3.4 Socio-economic Foresight towards setting National Plans

To foresight, a socioeconomic segment of any community means we need to understand the gaps between the current and future status and rising demands due to fast changes coming up in the next 10 to 20 years. Through such foresight, we can reform the socio-economic status towards a better-desired direction of tomorrow.

Most national plans of developing countries do not address social security properly while focusing on economic and political security. Thus, you see in a national plan as United Arab Emirates, or Bahrain, or Qatar the national plans to take into account economic growth of all the spectrum of society, regardless of the equal opportunities distribution between the different classes of society, Buheji (2018a). However, you would see that most of leading governments today are working on actions relevant to strategies that are linked towards a transformation to a defined future foresight of between 10 to 50 years. In certain countries as Norway, governments are working even on longer-term of prospective of 70-100 years from now. Such foresight analysis still short of the socio-economic details even if we study the national plans for developed countries, like Canada, Japan, Germany, France and Singapore.

The shortage of foresight socioeconomic status most probably would be due to not having the proper tool to realise such types of perspective due to low funding in this area. Governments need to annually allocate funding to conduct and update it actualised planned towards the foresighted socio-economic status in 10 years and more and set actions on how to overcome any possible crisis or gaps that undermine the community capacity to develop.

Therefore, an agreed national plan that brings in the collective local minds and efforts of government experts, the academics and scientists, the NGO and business leaders of any country is a must for any effective future socio-economic transformation. Heading to a future socio-economic status, or achievement, or milestone requires understanding the what and why before the how.

2.3.5 Importance of Socio-Economic Foresight on Re-Engineering our Wealth

Breaking or re-engineering of any old socio-economic system requires an understanding of the rituals and the norms that create the structures, or the mechanisms of such system and its related dynamic effect. This means we need to determine the drivers or the clusters that bring in such socio-economic status. Thus, government policy-makers can carry out national risk assessments that weigh the short to medium risks of the foresighted socio-economic disaster or disruption to human and economic welfare, to inform priorities for investment in preparedness and resilience.

One could imagine that the socio-economic risk landscape is shaped by major external and internal trends of known and sudden shocks. These shocks in this landscape will increase if the resources are not appropriately optimised. Having stress from the growing demand for natural resources, due to climate change, would just one example of this.

Hence, understanding the hidden and the unexploited opportunities of our real wealth and asset would reduce the pressures of our socio-economic crisis and would mitigate the effect of the rising frequencies or the severities of different disasters or their latter implications.

Any socio-economic study needs to carry the probabilities of a positive and negative scenario by 2030 and beyond. Then the national plan members need to determine the sequence of the authorities and society needed to prevent the realisation of negative scenarios. The actions should focus on eliminating socio-economic inhibitory factors. Hunt (2018).

Thus, any structured or unstructured re-engineering of socio-economic status would require two factors. First, a better understanding of the short- or long- term economic impacts of the abundant or scarce significant wealth of assets. Then, understand the natural influence of, for example, the environmental change, i.e. the influence of climate change, water scarcity, biodiversity loss, air pollution and the land-water-energy nexus.

2.4 Building Robust Resilient Socio-economic Models

2.4.1 Raising Socio-Economic Preparedness through 'Availability'

In order to foresight unique evolving socio-economic model from a crisis, we need to link it to a regional developing a strategy that maintains the stability of the social and cultural systems. This should help to develop a systematic methodology of scenario planning of social and economic developments, the minimum availability of socio-economic survival clusters needs to be established within the main sectors of the economy: the government, the civil society and the business community. Hunt (2018).

Through focusing on availability, we can stimulate creative thinking and trigger reforms in the institutional structures. Building preparedness in the institutional structures through foresight analysis, risk assessments and better availability frameworks could help to establish adaptive capacity in crisis management and besides it would demonstrate more accountability.

Learning to deal with current and long-term future socio-economic challenges, helps to shake-up the mindset and propose designing new approaches based on the availability of socio-economic competitiveness constructs. For example, dealing with the fairness of wealth distribution and relative poverty issues would ensure creating models that focus on 'inclusive economic growth'. This brings in better integration of different risks in socio-economic analysis.

Across countries, expert communities are increasingly engaged in horizon scanning and strategic foresight, carrying out projections of long-term socio-economic trends that affect national risk portfolios.

2.4.2 Utilising Resilience Economy for the Foresighted Socio-Economic Challenges

Rutter (2000) defines resilience as an act that requires the presence of clear substantial risk or adversity and which causes differentiates from normal or normative development. Resilience economy (RE), on the other hand, reflects the existence of life's purpose that would raise our capacity of solving problems and determining objectives and priorities when we, or our community, are faced with traumas or major changes in our life, such as facing sudden diseases, or war situations, or national crisis, or natural or human-made disasters that would negatively affect socio-economic life and its related activities.

If we target an economy that would have the ability to recover any socio-economic situation quickly, then we need this economy to be flexible and enabled, in order to bounce back after being adversely affected by a shock. Therefore, part of RE definition is its capacity to manage sudden or chronic fiscal deficits, or unexpected socio-economic outcomes.

Governments, civil and private sectors need resilience economy since it would give them greater ability to influence the socio-economy with minimal resources and ensures the functioning of their socio-economics through increasing their shock absorption capacity.

With RE being in the mindset and practices of the community, we can enhance the readiness for socio-economic transformation which allow us not just to survive the next disruptive challenge but also would develop it towards more stabilised socio-economy.

2.4.3 Building Socio-economically Resilient Communities

Resilience brings in the spirit of coexistence which is now proven to be one of the main sources for the reduction of the unequal distribution of classes within a society, which leads to an increase in poverty rates. Building socio-economically resilient communities can be achieved by three ways visualising proactive best practices, or actual mitigating risks, or learning from lessons and opportunities for improvement after the actual socio-economic crisis. Therefore, realising what is happening to the socio-economies in different countries, including learning from catastrophes due to failure in readiness are considered to be part of building socio-economically resilient communities. Yakwal et al. (2015).

In order for the communities to have the most resilient capacity which brings and sustain the balance between the different types of socio-economic programs in relevance to external, or internal shocks we need to measure here whether these capacities would be resilient enough (i.e. causing recovery and stability) to return the community to its initial state or better; using only minimal resources.

If RE embedded in the design the socio-economic related services and activities, it would affect the mental models through field assessment and implementation. This would create solutions driven by abundance thinking where we start to see the world as being full of opportunities and alternatives. This paradigm shift helps us to eliminate scarcity thinking, thus allowing us to see opportunities inside different problems and challenges.

Building a socio-economy that fully involves and engages humans needs a total people involvement (TPI) technique that depends on human equality and partnerships. However, when we increase this level of involvement and move it towards total people engagement (TPE) through having the people design, plan and execute socio-economic programs along with the decision-makers, then we can enhance the spirit of resilience and control the evil side of capitalism.

Although most capitalist countries in their economic system are fairly democratic in their political system, TPI could enhance the pillars of the socio-economic conditions in these countries too and protect their resilience development. However, with the subject coexistence in these countries, today with the increased influence of the extreme right parties are making TPI become very formal and non-value-added.

The effective use of TPI and TPE could improve really the resilience behaviour of the communities and make them more capable of what to emphasis towards creating better socio-economic living conditions. This could help to shift the paradigm towards the holistic wealth that integrates with the process of factual decision making. For example, to encourage any for-profit social organisations that support the role of the civic involvement in the socio-economy RE could be used to develop social control investments and funds that help to improve the economic development cycle again. This should help the socio-economic stakeholders to manipulate the forces of (supply vs demand), and change it towards utilising the (capacity vs demand).

2.4.4 Establishing Resilient Socio-Economy Family

Numerous studies focus recently on the role of family poverty to create more resilient family members. Studies, for example, have shown that some practices of poor parents help to promote socio-economic resilience within the family, Buheji and Ahmed (2019a). Even if a family goes through a divorce which eventually produces direct and indirect stress on their socio-economic status, the availability of resilience-based social support from the community can reduce the negative impact of stress on the family members and could yield positive socio-economic outcomes, such as producing entrepreneurs, or a productive family. Same would apply when the family would awake on the death of one of its family members. The community and its resilience mechanism would be the source of both recovery and maintaining a stable equilibrium which leads to both balance and harmony. Therefore, to establish resilient families, we must establish learning mechanisms that mitigate the effect of family disturbances and their influence on their socio-economic status. Resilient family relations would help to reorganize the changing patterns of functioning thus to adapt to their new situation, where many social analysts would agree that it helped maintain or improve their quality of life and general wealth. Buheji (2018b).

2.4.5 Transforming Middle Class from Passive Socio-Economies to Active Ones

Transforming any socio-economy from being a receiver of what is planned, i.e. passive socio-economy, as used to be during the peak of the industrial economy in 20th century, to a socio-economy where people would interact with lots of creativity and collaborations is not an easy task.

Developed and emerging economy nations have maintained a good history of the socio-economically active middle class, where they exhibit their capacity to be resilient to any socio-economic instability compared to people in developing and under-developed nations. The modern history, i.e. since the early 1900's, have shown that the main middle-class socio-economic concerns are ar0und both socio-political changes and sudden crisis in both the community and the country. This can be learnt especially from the events that have happened in the last half-century in countries in Africa and South America, where the increase in income inequality can be directly linked to the rise of both socio-political and socio-economic polarization.

2.4.6 Managing 4th Industrial Revolution Socio-Economic Challenges

Previous industrial revolutions provided more opportunities for the labour force and changed the quality of jobs. Those revolutions help to create a middle class that participated in the socio-economic development in every country. However, the current revolution works on abolishing the human functions and focus optimising the productivity of the factories that would increase the wealth and the benefits of the upper-class minority.

With Artificial Intelligence (AI), we could eliminate many human challenges, but also, we could increase other problems such as alienation of specific human communities which could cause socio-psychological problems. The latest rapid increase in the levels of depression and suicide

Are just one of the few signs of this new industrial development.

The 4th industrial revolution carries with it thus new types of poverty, that poverty in the ability to create effective decisions in comparison to AI Robots, which would limit our capacity to enjoy the wellbeing we are striving for.

2.5 Enhancement of Youth Capacity in Absorbing Socio-Economic Crisis

Cross-cultural studies have shown that youth participation in socio-economic tasks is a great enabler for solving socio-economic problems effectively. By enabling youth into the community socio-economic problem, we improve their self-esteem, enhance their moral development, increase their political activism and maintain their social relationships. Buheji (2019b), Buheji and Ahmed (2019b).

In education, if youth go through multi-disciplined teaching approaches that are built around socio-economic outcomes, their sustained engagement would be more guaranteed. With active experimentation or experiential learning, youth can start the curiosity journey of socio-economic problem solving with positive mindsets. This positive mindset would make youth manage the dynamic transformation stress exerted on them by the people, the resources, the institutions, and the systems.

Throughout history, we see that there are groups of the society that may be marginalized in the time of prosperity, and they are the one who suffers most in times of crisis. Many women and youth who live below the poverty line would be the most affected during the rising crisis. Buheji (2019b).

The need for youth had varied over the ages, when young people were a major force during wars, to periods when they became part of countries development advocates. As things have started to change and youth became the leaders of the economic change and the creators of ideas, besides the owners of wealth. However, this did not reduce poverty among young people.

2.6 Using Inspiration Labs in the Development of Socio-Economic Models

Social trends and socio-economic challenges usually would be studied in detail to be able to identify their problem. However, through the concept of Inspiration Economy, the inspiration lab sees challenges as sources of full opportunities that need to be discovered, or exploited. The latest financial European crisis, for example, teach us how to deal with socio-economic hyper-complexity, i.e. having many problems at the same time. i.e. being more interdependent from a single problem-solving approach. Astrov et al. (2018).

Inspiration labs go through community challenges and then develop ideas that are tested. Hence, through exploiting the hidden opportunities inside the socio-economic problem relevant to issues as in healthcare, education, community needs, youth and women empowerment; models are created. Buheji and Ahmed (2019b).

Many socioeconomic issues that might lead to future foresighted problems are also targeted in inspiration labs. For example, one certain socio-economic problem might lead to the rise of crimes, for example, investigating the process of how to eliminate the potential of such crimes would lead to the creation of a new model for other communities. From the work of both Kahneman (2011) followed by Thaler and Sunstein (2008), through targeting a model creation, we can even see how much we can create a more resilient mindset.

4.0 Research Methodology

Patton (2002) mentioned that in order to select the most appropriate methods for research we need to understand the resources available for conducting the study and the extent to which people in the field are accessible, besides the social context of the research. Upon the extensive literature review, this paper questions how the different dimensions of socio-economic issues tackled help to mitigate its development into a crisis in the future. The empirical part of this study draws on the qualitative case-study methodology of Eisenhardt (1989), which focus on interpretive methodology and thus allows theory and data to interact and influences methodological choices.

The socio-economic problems were extracted from Buheji (2018a), which listed cases of Inspiration labs. Then the projects were evaluated for both the probability of its occurrence and the hazard once it occurs. Based on this a socioeconomic foresight the project outcome is proposed. The selection of the projects was based on the probability of improving the outlook and moving from solving current problems to future problems.

5.0 Case Analysis and Findings

This paper aimed to identify the relationship between socio-economic issues and future foresight. The results show how we can transform socio-economic issues proactively, through models that would either mitigate a crisis, or prevent its occurrence, or learn from its outcome once it is over. The idea here is to ensure that we create sustainable models for the future foresighted crisis.

Ten cases were selected based on visualising the proactive best practices selected from the cases of the international inspiration economy projects, listed in Buheji (2018a). Then the cases were evaluated as to how the inspiration labs helped to mitigate their actual coming risks, or how they create learnings, or lessons and opportunities for improvement after the actual socio-economic crisis.

The case study analysis helps to build knowledge on how to transform the socio-economic issue proactively through models that would either mitigate a crisis, or prevent its occurrence, or learn from its outcome once it is over. This is achieved through understanding each case probability and hazard and then codifying its type of foresight lead.

Studying the 'probability' means understanding the level of the reality outcome that the specified socio-economic project managed to bring its targeted outcome, i.e. it had a clear influence on the community. While by understanding the 'hazard' of the case, we would appreciate the risks that might occur if the project was not executed, in the right time and place.

In Table (1) shows how the specific selection of inspiration labs tackled socio-economic issues are linked to specific probability and hazard that have three levels (high, medium and low). Based on the type of the calculated risk which comes from the results of Probability x Hazard, we can visualise the foresight of the socio-economic issue and prevent crisis (PC), or mitigate crisis (MC).

Table (1) Illustrates the probability of the influence of the Socio-economic issues and their hazards if not tackled in the right way and right time. The table defines what type of crisis foresight the Inspiration Labs (ILs) are helping us to achieve. i.e. what the specific type of lab is leading to? The framework is mainly only two identified crisis management tracks, either prevention of crisis (PC) or mitigation of crisis (MC).

Table (1) Links between Socio-economic Issues and Possible type of Crisis Management

Socio-Economic Issue tackled by ILs	Probability of its Influence	Hazard if not tackled	Type of Foresight
1. Raising Rural Communities & People in the Slums access to Education or basic life necessity schools	**High** (i.e. more people can access education and more types of education (formal and informal) found the less poverty variables would exist.	**High** (more drastic conditions of absolute poverty and people working in very poor conditions)	(PC)
2. Developing the Quality of Life of the Elderly (eliminating elderly homes and enhancing Geriatric Care Homes)	**High** (Longer quality of life and more integration between geriatric healthcare services and the family)	**High** -Majority of the population would not fully functional and would need more care. -We would have lonelier elderly people -Bigger gaps between generations as youth won't meet their grandparents	(PC)
3. Improving the contribution and the competitiveness of the retired by redirecting the investment of the pension funds	**High** - Maintain both the knowledge and the value of the retired	**Medium** We would witness more depression cases	(PC)

Socio-Economic Issue tackled by ILs	Probability of its Influence	Hazard if not tackled	Type of Foresight
4. Adopting multi-purpose public buildings for schools, healthcare centre and events gathering area	**Medium** - more utilization of building - better for the environment	**Medium** -Minimising the probability of more isolations	(MC)
5. Creating a Model of Poverty Elimination with minimal resources	**High** - Reduce the burden of targeting zero absolute poverty in developing or under-developed countries	**High** Minimise the speed of volatility of the marginalised communities	(MC)
6. Establishing Early Students micro start companies	**High** Entry to entrepreneurship would enhance the levels of innovation and creativity of youth	**Low** Spirit of entrepreneurs would stay something that is measured at later stages of life	(PC)
7. Enhancing the impact of 'woman development', not only 'women-empower.'	**High** - The progress of women who will help the progress of society	**Medium** Society would still see women as the weak part of the community	(PC)
8. Eliminating Water loss	**High** - The capacity to discover early the water leakages with minimal resources would ensure effective maintenance of clean water	**Medium** Water would be a more scarce resource.	(MC)

Socio-Economic Issue tackled by ILs	Probability of its Influence	Hazard if not tackled	Type of Foresight
9. Early detection of Non-Communicable Diseases (NCD's), i.e. Diabetes, Blood Pressure, Cholesterol and Obesity in the population without detailed examination	**High** - More quality of life - Fewer patients with complicated cases	**High** - More early death - More people with limited productivity	(MC)
10. Establishing Inspection' that minimize the rates of poisonous food with minimal intervention	**High** - More consumers trust and less incidents of food diseases	**Medium** Poisoning may increase due to lack of human immunity Resorting to supplements that have complications	(MC)

4.0 Discussion and Conclusion

4.1 Patterns of Resilience during Socioeconomic Crises

Since 2008, the world has been exposed to the socio-economic crisis that requires solidarity and psychological analysis. Developing socio-economic resilience frameworks by testing it through problem-solving labs helps to blend social, economic and cultural practices and the future foresighted challenges, and this could minimise the suffering from coming harmful or hazardous situations. Buheji (2018b).

This paper focused on sustainable patterns of both coping and adaption. Through the synthesis of the ten cases, we can see that inspiration labs and similar live labs could help to the foresight and work on many crises early and thus either prevent it or mitigate it once occurred. This resilience to socioeconomic crises needs to be supported by effective re-designing both the community cultural and social activities. Buheji (2018b).

Table (1) gives us a practical methodology for reviewing all the types of restrictions that chain our community's ability to deal with socio-economic problems early, or to work on what could bounce back any sudden on them. Managing to focus early on the socio-economic variables create a significant influence on managing and mitigating the risks of occurrences of severe recessions. It enhances the living and the learning from the socio-economic distortions, which could contribute to the vulnerabilities of the marginalised. Jing-Yu et al. (2018).

4.2 Benefits of initiatives as Inspiration Labs for bringing Foresighted Socio-economic Solutions

The most relevant aspect of this study is that it shows that the future socio-economic challenges can be foresighted. Practical field labs, as the international inspiration economy project (IIEP), inspiration labs (ILs), helps to develop the community capacity to deal with the future socio-economic crisis. Therefore, the paper calls indirectly for more such initiative as IIEP (ILs) that bring about realised positive socio-economic changes with clear, experienced outcomes. The researchers thus recommend that the reference models differentiate by initiatives and approaches as IIEP and ILs should be studied and developed further to help crack out any future human problems with minimal resources.

The approach that ILs projects bring could be generically carried by institutions, non-government associations, societies, private sectors, and then publicised through social media, books publications and scientific journals, so that many communities could avoid such future problems. The worked upon foresighted socio-economic problems could also be a source of development of communities and organisations and could help prevent the following types of poverty, complicated youth migration, slowness of quality of life and similar challenges.

4.3 Identifying Areas of Socio-economic Development

The main areas of any socio-economic challenges usually are only appreciated by the demographers who can detect issues like health and educational status, ageing and gender equality. However, the methodology presented in the case study and Table (1) shows that socio-economic challenges can be identified and measured through their level of probability of creating differentiated outcomes and their detrimental impact if not solved. Therefore, we say that sustainable socio-economic development requires effective availability and management of resources.

Through inspiration labs, we could outline the scenarios of how socio-economic variables or approaches may transform knowledge into products and services within different socio-economic frameworks. These bottom-up visions are then synthesised with different possible socio-economic frameworks conditions and megatrends, to extract the possible foreseen innovation.

Thus through realising the significant advances in the socio-economic status and linking its impacts to global challenges, we can evaluate total transformation requirements, including the costs of such transformation.

Through inspiration labs, the socio-economic transition can occur through the optimisation of the opportunities with the issue which can balance between the changes in the culture, the production and the consumption of resources. Through such a transition, we can reduce the negative influence of many coming foreseen and complicated socio-economic issues as migration, low fertility rates, changing family lifestyle, and urbanisation.

Reference

Anonymous (2019) Socioeconomic scenarios website
    https://www.nature.com/subjects/socioeconomic-scenarios

Astrov, V; Grieveson, R; Hanzl-weiss, D; Hunya, G; Jestl, S;
    Mara, I; Pindyuk, O; Podkaminer, L; Richter, S (2018)
    Socio-economic challenges, potentials and impacts of
    transnational cooperation in central Europe, The Vienna
    Institute for International Economic Studies
    https://www.interreg-central.eu/Content.Node/events/
    Policy-Brief-181018-full.pdf

Buheji, M (2019a) Shaping Future Type of Poverty - The Foresight
    of Future Socio-economic Problems & Solutions - Taking
    Poverty as a Context- Beyond 2030, American Journal of
    Economics, 9(3): 106-117.

Buheji, M (2019b) Youth Unemployment Mitigation Labs - An
    Empathetic Approach for Complex Socio-Economic Problem,
    American Journal of Economics, 9(3): 93-105.

Buheji, M (2019c) Understanding the Economics of Problem-
    Solving. A Longitudinal Review of the Economic Influence
    of Inspiration Labs- Three Years Journey on Socio-Economic
    Solutions. American Journal of Economics 2019, 9(2): 79-85

Buheji, M and Ahmed, D (2019a) The Intent – Shaping the
    future of Poverty Economy, AuthorHouse, UK.

Buheji, M and Ahmed, D (2019b) The Defiance - A Socio-
    Economic Problem Solving (Edited Book), AuthorHouse, UK.

Buheji, M. (2018a) Re-Inventing Our Lives, A Handbook for
    Socio-Economic "Problem-Solving", AuthorHouse, UK.

Buheji, M (2018b) Understanding the Power of Resilience
    Economy: An Inter-Disciplinary Perspective to Change the
    World Attitude to Socio-Economic Crisis, AuthorHouse, UK.

Graham, Y (2019) Ghana's socio-economic transformation and
    the imperative for equitable and inclusive development,
    social watch,

http://www.socialwatch.org/node/17507, Accessed date: 1/7/2019

Hunt A. (2018) Future Scenarios of Economic Development. In: Nicholls R., Hutton C., Adger W., Hanson S., Rahman M., Salehin M. (eds) Ecosystem Services for Well-Being in Deltas. Palgrave Macmillan, Cham.

Jing-Yu Liu, Shinichiro Fujimori, Kiyoshi Takahashi, Tomoko Hasegawa, Xuanming Su & Toshihiko Masui (2018) Socioeconomic factors and future challenges of the goal of limiting the increase in global average temperature to 1.5 °C, Carbon Management, 9:5, 447-457

Stylianidis, S. and Souliotis, K. (2019) The impact of the long-lasting socioeconomic crisis in Greece. *BJPsych international*, *16*(1), 16–18.

Yakwal, S; Bodang, J; Guyit, R (2015) Implementation of Inclusive Education for Nomadic Children with Disabilities in Nigeria: Implications for Guidance and Counselling, Asia Pacific Journal of Multidisciplinary Research, Vol. 3, No. 3, August.

YOUTH UNEMPLOYMENT MITIGATION LABS

An Empathetic Approach for Complex Socio-Economic Problem'8

[8]Buheji, M (2019) Youth Unemployment Mitigation Labs - An Empathetic Approach for Complex Socio-Economic Problem, American Journal of Economics, 9(3): pp. 93-105.

1.0 Abstract

Today many graduating youths would believe that the world is much harsher than what they thought, because they are constrained from smoothly entering the labour market. Therefore, youth unemployment is not only a United Nation Sustainable Development Goal (UN-SDG) but remains to be an important complex global challenge.

In this paper, we shall review all the past and contemporary approaches to solving the youth unemployment problem, in relevance to latest facts and then shall see the approach of a four years' socio-economic problem-solving approach, called the inspiration labs, and how it is tackling this issue from different perspectives.

The paper concludes with the calibration of the direction this UN-SDG challenge is handled all over the world.

Keywords: Youth Unemployment, Sustainable Development Goal (SDG), Youth Empowerment, Socio-economy, Problem Solving, Inspiration Labs, Inspiration Economy.

2.0 Introduction

Youth unemployment would continue to be a complicated problem as the world is still continuing its demographic shifts in developing countries. The problem of youth unemployment will continue to carry numerous domestic and global risks, including social exclusion, mass migration and generational gaps. Buheji (2018d)

At a time when young people in certain societies are being prepared as the engine of society and its sustainable resource.

Youth unemployment needs an economic, social and psychological approach more than a political approach. It is a security problem that carries with deep consequences towards poverty, deprivation and frustrations, which have profound effects on the level of quality of life of the community.

Unemployment affects both the psychological and the physical status of youth more than ever today. Studies show that the effects of unemployment stem from a sense of failure and loss of self-esteem, which raises the rate of silence that may lead some to commit a crime, drug abuse and even suicide.

In this paper, we shall explore the meaning of unemployment for youth specifically, besides modern unemployment statistics. Youth unemployment as a problem to be solved is discussed from different perspectives such as the current and required, such as education and recreation activities. Economic Discussion (2019).

Policies to reduce youth unemployment and the required policy reforms. Then a review for those youth not in education, not in employment and not in training, called for short (NEET). Then a review about the role of knowledge-based economy on the issue of youth unemployment is followed. Examples of youth unemployment challenges and the probability of youth staying unemployed shed light on the depth and the complexity of the problem. Buheji (2018e).

Then a case study of the way inspiration labs is tackling the youth unemployment a socio-economic problem and from different perspectives is explored. A comparative discussion on the contemporary efforts in tackling the youth unemployment issue in relevance to inspiration is evaluated and discussed, then recommendations for the way forward to close this major UN-SDG gap are suggested in conclusion. Amadeo (2018).

3.0 Literature Review

2.1 What is Youth Unemployment?

Unemployment can be defined as when an individual is hunting for employment and does not find a job or alternatives to a job, i.e. being self-employed. Unemployment is one of the major crises that happens around the world every era. Therefore, it is an issue that reflects the national or international economic status and the healthiness of investment potentials. Johansson and Handelshögskolan (2015).

The unemployment rate is measured by calculating the total unemployed individuals divided by the total number of the labour force in the country. As per the International Labour Organization (ILO,2012), there are more than 200 million globally or about 6% of the complete world workforce is unemployed. For youth, their unemployment differs even more if their NEET is high.

I.e. When youth are not in education and not work means we have a society a major wastage of both youth energy and spirit, Buheji (2018d).

2.2 Youth Unemployment Statistics

2.2.1 Statistics of Youth Unemployment in Modern History

The global unemployment rate reached a post during World War II to a high of 9.7% in 1982. With the economic recession, the unemployment rate reached 9.6% in the year 1983. It was in 1989 that the unemployment rate dropped to 5% but started enhancing again. This led to 6.8% in 1991 and 7.5% in 1992. Later and with the economic development, the unemployment rate fell to 6.9% in 1993, 4.5% in 1998 and to 4% in 2000; consequently. It was considered to be the lowest in the last three decades.

Since youth are essential to any economic development and growth, the drop-down in the overall global unemployment rate gave great hope for the ease of young people entry to the labour market, especially in emerging and developing market economies. This is especially true as the world reach approximately one-third of its working-age being youth. Buheji (2018d), Lagard and Bludorn (2019).

However, the reality today is the opposite. Still today youth, all over the world, face tough labour markets and job shortages. Approximately, 20% of 15- to 24-year-olds in the average emerging market and the developing economy are neither in work, nor in school (i.e. NEET); in comparison to 10% in advanced economies. Table (1) illustrates the percentage of youth unemployment selected developed and emerging economy countries, as per ILO (2015) statistics.

Table (1) Shows Youth Unemployment by Country

Country	% Youth Unemployment
Australia	13.2
Greece	50.6
France	25.4
India	18.1
Italy	43.9
Japan	7.2
Poland	23.2
South Korea	8.7
Spain	53.5
Turkey	19.5
United Kingdom	16.3
United States	12.4

Source: ILO 2015

The International Monetary Fund (IMF) published a report in (2019) that show that the share of youth, i.e. ages of 15-24 years, not in school and not in work, (NEET) in the past 13 years (from 2003 till 2016) stayed within 25-20% in emerging markets and developing countries, while in developed countries it stayed within 10%. Ahn et al. (2019) and Lagard and Bludorn (2019).

In Africa, youth unemployment is one of the growing problems in the continent and the world. It is of high importance, even more, today due to the migration crisis. According to the International Labour Organization (ILO), the unemployment rate among youth in Northern Africa was at 29.3% in 2016. (ILO, 2016). The situation in sub-Saharan Africa, specifically, is only slightly better where the youth unemployment rate was at 10.8% last year. In South Africa, more than half of all active youth were unemployed in 2016, representing the highest youth unemployment rate in the region. Buheji (2017b).

In Europe, the numbers are even worse. In general youth unemployment rates have reached in certain countries, about 50% on average. For example, in Spain youth unemployment rates reached (53.7%) and in Greece (50.7%), in Italy (42.9%), in Croatia (41.8%), in Portugal (35.5%), in Cyprus (34.9%) and Slovakia (28.5%). The lowest shown youth unemployment rate is in France (24.4%), then in Ireland (23.8%) and the same in Belgium.

WEF (2018) report warned that such sustained global financial crisis would create a "lost generation" and would hinder youth integration into traditional patterns of economic life. Among the specific issues raised by WEF report were the long-term youth unemployment; low-quality, part-time and temporary employment jobs. The WEF also pointed out the risk of weak links between education and worked; the impact of demographic change and migration; and the increasing pressures in relevance to social protection. WEF (2019).

WEF (2018) shows that youth unemployment has been broadly static since the publication of the WEF 2014 report, i.e. before the global financial crisis. Even where jobs creation has picked up since the crisis, concerns are rising about the growing prevalence of low-quality employment and the rise of the "gig economy".

In 2016, the UN launched the 'global initiative for decent jobs for youth' to coordinate policies on youth employment and young people's labour rights. The EU released €6 billion, as a youth jobs guarantee program, targeting to ensure that within four months of becoming unemployed young people are offered new employment, education, or a workplace apprenticeship.

2.2.2 Future Foresight of Youth Unemployment

Predictions say that youth unemployment will continue to rise in the following years. High unemployment has negative consequences on the economy of the country and population. More young people are expected to leave their countries of birth to find employment abroad.

The new IMF staff study shows that, if youth underemployment in the typical emerging market and developing economy were brought in line with the average advanced economy, the working-age employment rate would rise by three percentage points and economic output would get a 5% boost. IMF (2019) and Lagard and Bludorn (2019).

2.3 Youth Unemployment - Problems Solving

2.3.1 Youth Unemployment as a Problem

Unemployment as a problem can be solved in many ways and alternatives. Solving youth unemployment as a socio-economic problem can help to reduce the current total approaches of youth empowerment, Amadeo (2018). Most current approaches work to solve long-term youth unemployment is through ensuring better educational standards, launching of new empowerment programs, encouraging self-employment, entrepreneurship, ensuring access to basic education and reduction of the age of retirement. Buheji (2018a), Buheji (2018e).

Recently, most of the scientists see unemployment as an issue that could be solved when youth become creative, positive and competitive. This led to many initiatives that target to avoiding investing in unsuitable programs. Buheji (2018d).

Youth unemployment is another issue which is still happening in developed, underdeveloped and developing countries. There is major evidence that even the developed countries are battling with youth unemployment issues. The international labour organisation has mentioned the statistics of both employed and unemployed in 2012 which states that is about 6% of the world population are unemployed and youths are the ones who are unemployed, i.e. youth unemployment (ILO, 2012).

Many studies now show clear evidence that the delay in youth unemployment increases their likelihood of being unemployed in their later adult life (Gregg, 2001; Bell and Blanchflower, 2009). As a result, youth unemployment will also have a sustained impact on the level of wealth and growth in future periods.

Now officially, EU sees youth unemployment to be a serious problem even in Europe where the Eurostat (2015) shows the unemployed youth to be 22.1%, compared to 8.9% for the adult population. This figure shows the considerable difficulties that young people are facing when trying to access the labour market for the first time.

2.3.2 Education and Unemployment Problem

Education creates opportunities for young people that contribute to the fulfilment of their desires and the building of their personalities and the establishment of a secure and stable life. Education supposed to facilitate a better search for suitable jobs and opens the youth mindset to see opportunities in different ways. Therefore, many believe with their education certificates; they would get open doors of opportunities. Buheji, (2017c), WEF (2019).

The government should change the policies of requiring an expensive bachelor's degree, that take four to five years of one's life without real guaranteed employment outcome. Students should have more options to go to vocational school, or get a combination of liberal arts and then on-the-job training. Hence, it would be great to see companies start adopting apprenticeship programs, teaching young professionals what they need to know on the job. Ahn et al. (2019), Buheji (2018b), Buheji (2017a).

Boosting on human capital education and training are no longer an effective strategy to create employable youth, or labour productivity, nor does keeping high demand for the creation of new jobs. Reddy (2017). Part of the EU recent initiatives also is to improve educational attainment so that people can work in jobs requiring higher-level knowledge and skills. EU and national policies aimed at reducing school drop-out rates. WEF (2019).

The Active Labour Market Policy (ALMP) target to support youth employment and 'youth guarantee' schemes to ensure young people receive a job offer or continued education within a fixed period after leaving education, or becoming unemployed (European Commission 2014). This is supported with extended guidance to employment services created specifically to youth. This is also linked now to employers' social contributions (O'Higgins, 2010; Eurofound, 2011).

Now many students graduate with education fees debts on their shoulder.

Lack of diversified educational models that address the different youth vs market demands needs to lead to staying in confusion in the search for work and waiting for more than ten years without suitable or permanent work. The constraints for specialization increase the complexity of the problem of unemployment.

Despite their differentiated access to education, studies show that youth still suffer from inequality for jobs related to their welfare. Total unemployment could be valued at market prices, for example using young people's wage levels and average working hours, to provide a measure of wealth lost to the EU economy, because of youth underemployment in the same present period. For example, a recent Eurofound study has shown the estimated cost of young people who are not in employment, education or training (NEETs) in 26 of EU member states to be about €156 billion (representing 1.51% of EU's GDP) (Eurofound, 2012).

To reducing youth occupational immobility, many countries started apprenticeship schemes that aim to provide the unemployed youth with the suitable skills they need to find suitable employment and to make them attractive for a suitable job. For example, in 2013, over 500,000 people started apprenticeships in the UK.

Consistent with the increase in education is the decrease in the share of 16-21-year-olds in fulltime work (Barham, et al., 2009). Further, the evidence-base on particular transitions examines the impact of the constant growth of young people in temporary employment across the EU. This increased to about 42% of young people across the EU in 2010, compared to about 11% of those aged 25–59 (Eurofound, 2014).

The recent (EU Commission, 2014) report shows the increased focus on improving the skills of young people to meet employers' demands better and to reduce the mismatch between available vacancies and job seekers by supporting vocational learning in apprenticeships, traineeships and placements and introducing quality standards for vocational education. Thus funding more apprenticeships and workplace learning are now a top priority for EU countries (EMCO, 2011; ILO, 2011; O'Higgins, 2010; European Employment Observatory, 2010).

2.3.3 Youth Sport and Unemployment Problem

Today youth-focused sports contribute to absorbing the burdens of disturbance resulting from unemployment disruption. By integrating youth into a social and cultural atmosphere, while contributing to the building of youth's personality and spirituality, we can transform the energy into balanced and productive work, thus preventing deviation and mental illness.

Through Improving the situation of many millions of young Europeans failing to find gainful employment, and more generally suffering from deprivation and social exclusion, has to be a priority for policy-makers' initiatives.

2.3.4 Influence of Youth Unemployment Problem

The problem of youth unemployment can influence the stability of national insurance contributions to society. The level of financial support expenditure for apprenticeships and internships would be influenced too.

Employed youth can reduce occupational mobility and thus, knowledge capital leakage. Also, a well-established employment program would help to improve geographical mobility and thus to cause improvement for the minimum wages. Once youth are employed, the community would avoid the risk of the poverty trap.

In 2012, 42.1% of young people across the EU were on a temporary contract which was four times the rate for adult workers (Eurofound, 2013). This shows the gap that youth unemployment does.

Now it is an accepted trend and fact that full-employment does not mean zero unemployment! There will always be some frictional youth unemployment which may be useful to have a small surplus pool of labour available. Most economists argue that there will always be some frictional unemployment of perhaps 2-3% of the labour force.

Amadeo (2015) seen that economic growth rate of 2-3 per cent can create only a maximum of 150,000 jobs which is not enough to prevent high youth unemployment, especially with the high influx of graduates. When unemployment creeps above 6-7 % and stays there, it means the economy can't create enough new youth jobs also.

2.4 Policies to Reduce Youth Unemployment

2.4.1 General Policies to Reduce Youth Unemployment

Many policies are usually released to reduce youth unemployment. For example, the low-interest rates and improving credit supply to businesses, besides depreciation in the exchange rate to help exporters is part of the story.

Other indirect youth unemployment policies were the infrastructure investment projects, reductions in corporation tax (to increase investment), spending more incentives for research and innovation that would encourage new business start-ups.

Most countries in the world have moved their policy to rapidly support small and medium enterprises (SME's) because of their inability to create new jobs. New policies now focus on SMEs approaches that target to transform the educated youth to be a major source of innovation and economic empowerment. Other policies, as the productive families' empowerment policy, helped to create the right conditions for youth to start their jobs as part of the family. Such policies help youth to create the right source of income and training to enter the labour market through self-employment projects. Buheji (2018a)

Recent EU reform policies and programmes (Eurofound 2012, Berlingieri et al. 2014, O'Reilly et al. 2015) aim to review the employment protection legislation in relevance to minimum wages to encourage companies to take on more young people. (Eurofound, 2011; O'Higgins, 2010).

2.4.2 Policies that Encourage Self-employment

Johansson and Handelshögskolan (2015) studied why some youth become self-employed instead of wage or salary earners upon returning to employment, using Finnish microdata and a multinomial logit model.

To close the unemployment gap, the European Union established a SALTO-YOUTH program which is a network of six resource centres working on European priority areas within the youth field. Hence, self-employment policies have shifted the focus of the government towards subsidising the cost of the new start-ups. European Union (2019).

As the dependency ratio is increasing in almost all the developed countries and leading developing countries, government policies need to re-evaluate its expenditures on social security or social insurance program and focus on empowering or developing youth for creating more their markets or meeting the demands of the dynamics of the market. Young people are highly needed today to enter the labour market as self-employed, as early as possible, as they can help in managing to pay for the huge numbers of those retiring. Buheji (2018a)

Evans and Leighton (1989) report that the salary youth that has entered self-employment on average have more experience than those not entering self-employment. Studies indicate that in the U.S. youth that suffers from longer duration of unemployment were more likely to enter self-employment.

The more we have concrete self-employed projects that would help to reduce youth unemployment this would influence the functioning of the labour market and would enhance the investment of youth in education and development (European Commission 2014a and 2014b) and Johansson and Handelshögskolan (2015).

2.5 Key barriers to Lowering Unemployment

There are many key barriers to lowering the unemployment issue. For example, high levels of long-term youth structural unemployment in the UK was found to be due to the complex welfare benefits, or low paid jobs that keep families in relative poverty. WEF (2019).

Studies show that one of the barriers of unemployment is that they are being stuck on part-time jobs. Other barrier found to be due to the continuous gap and variations in education outcomes or having low levels of educational achievements. Ahn et al. (2019).

Other barriers to reducing unemployment are the inequality for young women who usually influenced by negative economic conditions more than young men. Parental education was found to affect young people's employment transitions significantly.

2.6 Youth not in Education, Employment or Training (NEET) as part of the Unemployment Problem

NEET is very important to measure the effectiveness of youth employment approaches in any country or community. Although they remain in a precarious labour market status and at risk of social exclusion during their participation in such programmes, they would not be classified as NEET. For example, youth unemployment rates, despite being available for all EU member states, or rates of young people 'Not in Employment, Education and Training' (NEET) as a percentage of the total resident population of the age group, depend to a large extent on the characteristics of the education system (Eurofound, 2012).

A study was carried in the UK, by the National Statistics Office (2016), showed that NEET is an issue in 90% of the member states starting with countries as France, Greece, Spain and Italy where its proportion ranges between 25% and 30% of young people who an immigrant/minority background, or living in disadvantaged areas. Many of these youth NEETs vary considerably across the EU, between 4.4% of all young people in the Netherlands to 21.8% in Bulgaria (Eurofound, 2012).

Studies show that to manage the challenge of NEET, the school-to-work transition, need to be redesigned, including the transition from further education colleges to the labour market,

Crawford et al. (2011). Crawford and his team carried a similar longitudinal study on the UK and found generally that the trend of youth continuation in education enrolment of ages 16- to 21. However, the average youth employment rate slightly declined, and the use of fixed-term contracts increased, while the share of 16-year-olds who were not participating in education fell.

To improve the inclusion in the labour market and human capital accumulation while reducing segmentation and transitions from school to NEET; The European Commission has released selected indicators to monitor the field of youth NEET policy. A 'Dashboard of 40 EU Youth Indicators' (European Commission, 2011) was produced in March 2011, listing: Education/Training; Employment and Entrepreneurship; Health and Well-Being; Social Inclusion; Culture and Creativity; Youth Participation; Volunteering; Youth and The World.

2.7 Youth Unemployment as a Global Issue in Knowledge Economy

The issue of unemployment is very silly in an age with knowledge supposed to be the currency and new trend. It requires the cooperation of regional and national institutions, an in-depth analysis of the problem and the active participation of everyone. Although EU development in the knowledge-based economy; Quintini and Martin (2006) found that between 1995 and 2006 on average youth unemployment fell across OECD countries, however, it improved in more than half of the countries but severely deteriorated in a few.

We live in a digital age where modern communication technology has shaped our world, and it has impacted our lives tremendously and is supposed to solve the world's biggest problems. For example, Singularity University in the US is teaching people how to leverage exponential technology to impact 1 billion people positively. This is a knowledge-based era where youth impact can be tremendous if they are well utilised and appreciated. Economic Discussion (2019).

Hence, the more youth are employed with the mindset of minimising material consumption and focus on production that integrates knowledge in the output, the more possibilities they are expected to get. Due to this change, intellectual labour youth is needed more today in the labour market to re-evaluate the productive age and help towards effective transformation. It is a generation that could benefit more from good technology infrastructure and highly connected mobility business with low-cost internet connections, if employed and their productivity optimised at the right time. Buheji (2018c)

With youth continuing not to be employed in the right time and place, we would still have youth not being connected to mobile devices which means a greater loss of potential opportunities. Despite this fact, there are more than half a billion people across Africa now subscribe to mobile services, despite it being the highest continent in poverty. Buheji (2017c).

With the rapid evolution of the technology and the demand for a digitally skilled workforce, we call for short today the App generations, governments and education authorities need to adapt to the fast change based on this technology in the education system. This adaptation capacity would reflect on the compatibility of youth to the fast-changing market demands. Eshelman (2015), Buheji (2018b).

2.8 Examples of Youth Unemployment Challenges

To shed an example of the type of youth unemployment challenges, a review of the published literature about east, west and middle of the world was explored. In the United Kingdom, for example, youth employment found to happen only when there is sustained economic growth. Reducing cyclical volatility in relevance to youth requires a UK balanced growth. This found to affect even the education investment.

In the USA, youth unemployment is three times ahead of the elders. The youth unemployment rate is above 5.7%, and about 17% of the nation's youth are jobless. WEF (2019).

In Korea, the study of Kim (2019) mentioned about the most sought-after careers among teenagers and young adults in South Korea are becoming government jobs. This is due to the slowing down of the Korean economic growth in export-driven industries. Kim mentioned about 10 million of graduating youth in the next five years are considering risk-free government jobs.

Unemployment among those Koreans of ages 15 to 29 reached 11.6% last spring. It is a level where the Korean president called to be catastrophic, compared what used to be between 3% and 4% just a few years ago. Analysts say part of the problem for young job seekers in South Korea is the widening gap between the quality of jobs at family-owned conglomerates like Samsung and LG and the rest of the players, due to global economic slow.

In Algeria, Yahia (2018) carried a study about the evolution of the unemployment rate and growth rate in Algeria during the period 1970- 2015. The overall unemployment rate in Algeria has declined considerably over the last decade falling from 28.3% in 2000 to 9.4% in 2015.

The first analysis indicates that this Algerian unemployment decline was due in particular to the public investment programmes implemented in the period 2000-2015. This public employment programs created about 6.25 million jobs between 1999 and 2008. This economic growth has probably contributed to the fall in youth unemployment, real GDP growth increased from 3% in 2001 to 7.2% in 2003 and 5.9% in 2005, followed by a sharp slowdown in 2006 and 2007 to around 1.7% and 1.6% respectively, partly because the surge in international oil prices affected domestic demand. Howeverm Yahia (2018) reported that the unemployment rate in Algeria (9.4% in 2015) remains high compared to other the Middle East and North Africa (MENA) countries. For instance, in 2014, the unemployment in Iran is 10.6%, Morocco 10.2%, Turkey 9.2%, MENA countries 8.8%, Venezuela 7%, Indonesia 6.2%, Saudi Arabia 5.6%, Russia 5.1%, China 4.7%, Nigeria 4.8%. Yahia (2018).

Hadjivassiliou et al. (2015) examined labour market performance affecting young people in the light of recent policies in Europe, drawing on an analysis of EU Labour Force Survey data 2004-2012. Hadjivassiliou and his colleagues developed a single index measure of labour market performance combining nine variables of labour market inclusion, human capital formation, labour market segmentation and transitions out of education. The idea was that one index would show the performance in relevance to employment capacity and especially youth. No EU Member States achieved full 100 per cent performance on individual dimensions, for example avoiding entirely unsuccessful transitions out of school or achieving full employment of the 15-24-year-olds. The index can be interpreted as measuring the shortfall of achievement across the four key dimensions of inclusion, human capital formation, labour market segmentation and transitions out of the education.

Hence institutional change is needed to create effective outcomes in factors associated with young people's labour market transitions.

2.9 Probability of Youth Staying Unemployed

When we compare unemployed youth probability of moving into a wage or salary work with the probability of moving to self-employment, we find that married youth individuals, individuals with longer unemployment spells, individuals with more self-employment experience, and individuals with more wealth are more likely to become self-employed instead of taking a wage or salary job upon becoming reemployed. Johansson and Handelshögskolan (2015).

To anticipate the results, we find that a long spell of unemployment increases the probability of entering self-employment from unemployment when compared to entering paid employment from unemployment. This also holds after controlling for previous self-employment experience.

In countries with large-scale apprenticeship systems, such as Germany and Austria, youth have less possibility of staying unemployed. Youth apprentices are included in the total labour force, because vocational education and training (VET) are delivered primarily by firms.

However, unemployment as a percentage of the total labour force in countries with college-based VET is likely to be upward-biased because of the understated denominator (total labour force). In apprenticeship countries, youth unemployment probability risks are understated because the total labour force includes all people in VET.

Many youths have the right skills to find fresh work, but factors such as high house prices and housing rents, family and social ties and regional differences in the cost of living make it difficult and sometimes impossible to change the location to get a new job. Many economists point to a persistently low level of new house-building as a major factor impeding labour mobility and the chances of finding new work.

In order to reduce the possibility of youth staying unemployed for long times, many governments subsidies for businesses that take on the long-term unemployed – for example, as part of the UK youth contract, payments of up to £2,275 are available to employers who take on young people (aged 18-24) who have been claiming JSA for more than six months. The same thing in Bahrain were employed in specific industries would get more than half of the national youth salary for the first two years. In certain countries in Europe, there is a scheme that would help to lower the tax on businesses that employ more youth or support the employer national insurance contributions.

In the last one decade, many developing countries have started to follow the EU programs which encourage entrepreneurship and innovation as a way of creating new products and market demand, which could generate new employment opportunities?

3.0 Methodology

Youth unemployment is a tragedy that is no one's fault in particular. It's a political problem. It's an economic problem. And it's a societal problem. Here are three solutions that try to tackle youth unemployment from a few different angles.

The current approaches for youth unemployment are synthesised to be either proactive or reactive approaches. Then these current approaches are compared to the published approaches of Inspiration Labs and how it addresses youth unemployment as a socio-economic problem. A holistic, practical solution is extracted from both the synthesis of the current literature and latest labs regarding mitigation of youth unemployment as a proactive way to avoid a foresighted crisis.

4.0 Case Study

The international inspiration economy project, which started in September 2015 focused on different socio-economic problems, like poverty, women advancement, youth migration and quality of life. One of the repeated problems solved, through models only is the mitigation of youth unemployment, which is called 'Youth Unemployment Mitigation Labs'. The idea of these labs was to reduce youth unemployment or its negative influence through proactive models that could help to solve the complexity of this mega socio-economic problem. Buheji (2018e).

The following list of Table (2) shows the different socio-economic problems or challenges solved in relevance to youth unemployment and the mitigation approaches followed in the different communities, countries visited and in different situations.

Most of these socio-economic solutions have detailed stories behind them, as what is the causes of the youth unemployment and why and how it is created or influence; which is beyond the purpose of this paper. Many of these projects were carried out in Bahrain, Bosnia & Herzegovina, Slovenia, Morocco, Mauritania and most recently in India. Hence, it can't be compared to the many and long efforts of many countries in relevance to impact, however, it can be matched for the effectiveness of the approaches taken it is being new possibilities for closing the youth unemployment gap effectively and efficiently.

Table (2) List of Youth Unemployment Mitigation Labs carried out by the researcher from September 2015 till March 2019.

a)   Direct Youth Unemployment Proactive Approaches (DP)

Type of Business	Summary of Socio-Economic Type of Inspiring Projects/Models
1. Education for job creators & capacity building for job seekers (DP)	1 - Developing creative thinking programs. 2 - Discovering Inspiring Students at the right time during their 12 years in education. (Early inspiration discovery program). 3 - Establishing track of the inspired students after graduation (Inspiration Pathways). 4 - Delivery of (extra-curricular programs). 5 - Establishing early inspiration discovery program. 6 - Building Inspiration resources within School and after School. 12 - Establishing Future Boundary-less Schools

Type of Business	Summary of Socio-Economic Type of Inspiring Projects/Models
2. High Education that creates new labour market (DP)	1 - Build a knowledge economy driven practices, including implementation of Lifelong learning skills programs 2 - Improve the academic counselling that enhance the students' graduation time and give proper guidance at the right time. 3 - Improve the University capability to attract competitive projects and contracts through re-organising its knowledge expertise and profile. 4 - Establish better readiness for students lifelong learning skills as per type of speciality and disciplines. 5 - Enhance students' fitness or competence to meet labour market demand. 6 - Ensure students finish the requirements of the curriculum in the planned time: i.e., within four years for Bachelor programmes, and one and half years for Masters programmes. 7 - Apply Pull-thinking technique to improve academic advisory services. 8 - Apply 'smart registration practices' that enhances the students' choices and eliminate waste in opening extra sessions.
3. Labour Market (DP)	1 - Shifting Unemployment through inspiring the stratification of Human Capital data and building models in specific industries as per countries sustainable socio-economy needs 2 - Minimising unemployment rate through effective counselling 3 - Raising opportunities for employment through sourcing type of job opportunities, especially in less demanding jobs 4 - Improving locals' employment and demand in areas of hospitality, engineering and nursing 5 - Minimise the gap between locals and expat in the main jobs of market demand by defining areas that the national labour should compete.
4. Improving handcrafts in Villages (DP)	Improving the quality of handcrafts finishing and representation in the villages.

Type of Business	Summary of Socio-Economic Type of Inspiring Projects/Models
5. Village Society – Productive Families & Eco-Tourism Program (DP)	1 - Collection of small and large projects that target to create a comprehensive eco-tourism village. 2 - All projects related to working from home and the provision of raw materials to making gift products, fashion design are inter-related, and this gives more importance to the project. 3 - Target is to gradually make the village reach tourist spot with different hospitality activities especially during holidays and specific seasons
6. Graduating and Unemployed Graduate Students Mindset Management (DP)	1 - Understanding Dynamics of Labour Market 2 - Setting life purposefulness Mindset 3 - Challenging transformation towards self-independence and 'Big Picture' Legacy Model 4 - Enhancing Employer engagement with schools, colleges and universities and improve the feedback Students interaction and readiness to challenges of the local economy.
7. Women Entrepreneurship NGO (DP)	1 - Analysing the impact of programs on 'woman development', not only 'women-empower', and the 'living standards' that comes with the 'Quality of Life' in the NGO area and scope of delivery. 2 - Optimising the inter-disciplinary learning approach. 3 - Enhancing the 'learning by doing' practices 4 - Measure the differentiation of women on the economy.
8. Organic Farming Tourism (DP)	Select areas of Organic Farming and turn it around eco-tourism to enhance the young formers profit margin and quality of life while supporting family continuity and encouragement of youth into this business.
9. Social Insurance (DP)	1 - Creating selective thinking in the way of investment of pension fund that would enhance the productivity of the national economy 2 - Inspiring the social responsibility plans to ensure that selective type of lower pension jobs is more prepared for entrepreneurship after retirement.

Type of Business	Summary of Socio-Economic Type of Inspiring Projects/Models
10. Applied Science Colleges (DP)	1 - Inspiring students to enhance their scientific and research contribution towards innovation index by more focused projects 2 - Use the power of peer to peer influence to improve non-performing students
11. Woman Village NGO (DP)	1 - Enhance the Return on Capital Employed for the villagers during the chain of making to delivery and distribution 2 - Enhance young girls' involvement in Woman village activities to ensure the sustenance of knowledge transfer.

Source: Buheji, M. (2018) Re-Inventing Our Lives, A Handbook for Socio-Economic "Problem-Solving", Appendix (2) AuthorHouse, UK.

b)   Indirect Youth Unemployment Proactive Approaches (IP)

Type of Business	Summary of Socio-Economic Type of Inspiring Projects/Models
12. Radio & TV – Bahrain & Bosnia (IP)	1 - Build focused positive psychology waves of initiatives that raise the aspiration of the society and trust of the future of the socio-economy of the country 2 - Setting inspiration & youth economy focused strategic programs that integrate all the concerned parties towards action

Type of Business	Summary of Socio-Economic Type of Inspiring Projects/Models
13. Social Development to mitigate Unemployment Risks (IP)	1 - Improving the Quality of Life of the Elderly/ Geriatric Care Homes through exploring social asset of Day-Care Homes, instead of permanent residency homes. 2 - Inspiring the capacity of the productive family program to be more self-independent and attractive for more family members to join as full-time employees/ owners. 3 - Building stronger family businesses that have higher Return on Capital Employed (ROCE). 4 - Enhance the return from Elderly homecare production 5 - Enhance the quality of life of the Disabled People and their Production 6 - Easing the process of home care 7 - Supporting 'Working from Home' Program 8 - Revaluating the Capability of Social Allowance Value and Entitlement – in relevance to Quality of Life with priorities. 9 - Enhancing the quality and competitiveness of the product of the Retired & the Disabled 10 - Improving the Quality of Micro-Start Families with a focus on Women and People Vulnerability. 11 - Improving Quality of Life of Families in isolated communities and tribes (enhance the productivity factors for women and families working from home), with a target to reduce the impact of poverty through eco-tourism projects.
14. Quality Assurance in Education (IP)	1 - Ensuring that all students in under-performing school meet the minimal standard. 2 - Ensure that QA system create job creators, not job seekers

Type of Business	Summary of Socio-Economic Type of Inspiring Projects/Models
15. Woman National Planning (IP)	1 - Setup a comprehensive outcome and legacy-driven national plan that changes the way woman are empowered in Bahrain by giving her more accountability to create social cohesion, stability and national competitiveness. 2 - Closing the gap and accelerating the transformation towards 'Women Development' instead of 'Women Empowerment' after five years from the National Plan Kick-off. 3 - Ensure knowledge sharing between Business Women, Women Entrepreneurs and Women of Productive Families Programs and especially those of the same or relevant business and link it to gamification rating. (i.e. Rating of Entrepreneurs who contribute and share knowledge)
16. Humanitarian Services Agency (NGO's) (IP)	1 - Reversing the model of poverty support, by making poverty as a temporary condition that we need to prepare the beneficiaries to beyond this stage. 2 - Diverting the type of services to be more for sustained income, instead of non-sustainable support 3 - Mapping partnership collaboration services (Academic, youth, NGO's, Government, etc.) - Building Cost and Profit centre
17. Socio-Economic Role of School Dormitory (IP)	1 - Showing the benefit and the differentiation of the 'Non-Performing Students' towards the Society and the Socio-Economy. 2 - Establishing Students micro start companies 3 - Establishing model for dealing non-performing students 4 - Showing the self-independence of Religious Studies schools and students (by developing more profit rather than cost centre).
18. University (IP)	Ensuring Lifelong Learners Students through the inspiring way of flipped class teaching and ensuring suitable preparedness for coming life challenges.

Type of Business	Summary of Socio-Economic Type of Inspiring Projects/Models
19. Municipalities and Urban Development (IP)	1 - Redesigning the public buildings for schools, hospitals to create more multi-purpose buildings owned by the Government and measured for its rate of occupancy and utilisation. 2 - Enhance recycling culture and practices, besides prove its financial benefits for decision-makers, without increasing resources. 3 - Improve Building maintenance facilities in the early stages of government-owned building designs
20. Tender Board (IP)	1 - Diverting more tenders to the benefit of local SMEs and new start-ups. 2 - Setting performance standard for the role of the tender board in the cycle of the economy.
21. Inspiration Economy Teaching Program in Higher Education (IP)	1 - Implementation of Inspiration Economy Diploma Program 2 - Illustration by Doing Multi-disciplinary teaching in classes 3 - Illustration of how inspiration economy changes the way Course intended learning outcome and the program intended learning outcome through techniques as changing the enablers (i.e. the way teaching is delivered in flip class approach where students teach, and the teacher facilitates) 4 - Establish outcomes that are measured by 'open book exam' and by effective projects that enhance the students persistent in creating positive change in the area studies.
22. Management of NGO's role in creating better Socio-Economies (IP)	1 - Creating Discussion Group between the different last three generations that identifies: the respected difference, the gaps and positivity of intergeneration gap. 2 - Setting projects for mitigation of the gaps

Type of Business	Summary of Socio-Economic Type of Inspiring Projects/Models
23. Greenhouse project in eco-tourism villages (IP)	1 - The project involves many people from the village and youth to produce semi high-end products relevant to what the greenhouse produces. 2 - Branding, Packaging, Labelling and Marketing of the semi high- end products of the eco-village. 3 - Reduce Migration of Youth with more employment opportunities for the villager's families.
24. 'Education on Wheels' & 'Education at Door Steps' Projects (IP)	1 - Target to deliver education to rural and isolated communities. 2 - Formal and Informal Education for children in slums areas.
25. Agriculture and Farming (IP)	1 - Redesign Bahraini farmers' produce by establishing what is called "National Farmers' Day." 2 - Improve the distribution chain of local salad by attracting consumers to purchase local vegetables and fruits, and arranging deals between hospitality suppliers and local farmers. 3 - Increase Palm Trees implantation by the government, private and the public. 4 - Increase Palm tries protections, care, production and by-product industry develop 5 - Improve the level of Gardening Competitions
26. Improve learning capacities to lifelong learning citizens on activities (IP)	1 - Show influence of Disruptive Education and Multi-discipline on creating more inspiring students 2 - Simulation experiments & hands-on to enhance community innovation around the university campus.

Source: Buheji, M. (2018) Re-Inventing Our Lives, A Handbook for Socio-Economic "Problem-Solving", Appendix (2) AuthorHouse, UK.

c) Direct Youth Unemployment Reactive Approaches (DR)

Type of Business	Summary of Socio-Economic Type of Inspiring Projects/Models
27 - Psychiatric Services that help mitigation of un-employment Risks (DR)	1 - Inspiration of capacity to manage the anxiety to avoid reaching the level of chronic anxiety 2 - Reduce the need to treat anxiety with medicines. 3 - Reduce suicide ratio due to early treatment of main causalities among youth. 4 - Reduce the patients' sick leave due to self-assessments of psycho-sematic symptoms
28 - Commercial Sector (DR)	1 - Enhancement of CR registration through inspiring the reality of 'one-stop-shop'. 2 - Improving the contribution of Microstate and Small Enterprises towards more profitability and enhancing its actual contribution to Labour Market. 3 - Improving the speed and availability of fine stones and pearls test certificates 4 - Improving the cash flow status of Family Enterprises and reducing bad debts 5 - Improving the smooth transition of businesses from 2nd to 3rd generations. 6 - Building Independent Business Models 7 - Ensuring 2nd generation appreciates the importance of family business governance 8 - Raising the capacity, the differentiation of the 2nd generation 9 - Setting the smooth transition mechanisms within the families generations.
29 - Pension Fund (DR)	Inspiring investment towards enhancement Local Market Stability

Type of Business	Summary of Socio-Economic Type of Inspiring Projects/Models
30 - Labour Fund (DR)	1 - Ensuring that all funded projects had made a success story through the domino's effect of Labour Funds. 2 - Ensure measurement of success stories in relevance to Labour fund projects 3 - Ensuring the developing capacity in the survival of start-ups of more than three years on average and development of safe exits to youth projects. 4 - Minimise enterprises' dependency on government aid funds. 5 - Divert more mentorship on 'Necessity Entrepreneurship' and improve the solutions they bring to the community.
31 - Migrants & Migration Risks Mitigations (DR)	1 - Program for healing migrants' psychology and mental healthiness to create from them contributing citizens in the hosting country. 2 - Help establishing special Entrepreneurship Companies (using collaborative & knowledge economy techniques) for Migrants youth that accelerate their preparedness for inclusion in the new labour market. 3 - Create success stories of sharing economy based models of migrants who came back to re-settle and influence their socio-economy. 4 - Enhance migrants' productive families' capability integration in the country of the host.
32 - Barbarian farmers Village (DR)	1 - Improving the quality of life of families in the Amazigh Villages through eco-tourism and small family businesses that support such cluster 2 - Build youth independence program that counters poverty through raising the capacity of the farmers for competitive packaging and distribution. 3 - Build youth trust in the village system as a source of income

Type of Business	Summary of Socio-Economic Type of Inspiring Projects/Models
33 - Students Socio-psychology Awareness and counselling programs (DR)	1 - Sponsoring project on counselling the students' social workers and councillors 2 - Simplify tools for measuring students' safety or positive psychology or stress release 3 - Not our goal to do students awareness campaign for universities, but do projects make a university or school bullying, harassment, etc. 4 - Tackle issues of students' depression and see its influence on society.
34 - Ministry of Labour (DR)	1 - Re-Engineering Counselling Services to start from High School and be Flexible towards Job Creators than just Job Seekers. 2 - Ensuring alternative plans for graduating specialities with constraint opportunities 3 - Starting Companies for Unique Jobs as Nursing, Social Workers, Hospitality Services. 4 - Nationalising Jobs that represent the country heritage and support tourism 5 - Exploring the possibility of creating Human Capital Bank that would transform 30% of the Job Seeker towards job creation; over a planned career path. 6 - Closing the Gender Gap in Unemployment, by re-inventing new productivity jobs for Graduating Women.

Source: Buheji, M. (2018) Re-Inventing Our Lives, A Handbook for Socio-Economic "Problem-Solving", Appendix (2) AuthorHouse, UK.

d)   Indirect Youth Unemployment Reactive Approaches (IR)

Type of Business	Summary of Socio-Economic Type of Inspiring Projects/Models
35 - Bringing Low Privileged Community Children to Formal-Education by focusing on Sports (IR)	1 - Integrating youth with both formal sport and traditional games 2 - Evaluate possibility for the continuation of formal and informal education 3 - Use peer to peer education
36 - Housing Services (IR)	1 - Reduce the gap between citizens' demands and their quality of life needs 2 - Improving the choices and variety of options in non-villa packages (i.e. flats) 3 - Reduce the negative social inequality and improve social coexistence through post-housing services

Type of Business	Summary of Socio-Economic Type of Inspiring Projects/Models
37 - Societal Change Programs (IR)	1 - Mitigation of Migration amongst Youth 2 - Optimise the Youth Quality Life through Students Pull thinking targeted programs 3 - Building a poverty blockage and prevention program 4 - Addressing the Gambling (pitting) behaviour amongst youth and building prevention scheme through schools' model 5 - Building Youth Entrepreneurship & Innovation programs 6 - Enhancing Youth contribution in voluntary work through rectifying and supporting a change in Sports club towards enhancing youth decision making. 7 - Bridging the gap between academic Social Work and Social Studies Schools and the realised community problems. (Building Life-Long Learning Programs that shape the Community) 8 - Improving disserted women shelters returns. 9 - Improving children without known parents' programs 10 - Enhancing Red-Cross Programs Impact in the positive psychology of the community 11 - Improving Pre-School influence programs on Children of Homeless and Beggars' families.
38 - Camel Wool Carpet Factory to be in Villages (IR)	1 - Reverse-Design for Camel Wool Factory-Production from the Factory to Production to the Factory 2 - Re-Distribute Manual Wool Carpet Machines from Factory focused on Villages & Production Families Focused. 3 - Re-establish Organic Handmade Carpet Marketing Program

Type of Business	Summary of Socio-Economic Type of Inspiring Projects/Models
39 - Improve the Quality of Life of 'Waste Pickers' (IR)	1 - Improve Quality of Life of 'Waste Pickers' Families through differentiating their productivity from Municipalities coming to Waste Management 2 - Segregating waste bins implantation in universities, schools & hotels, residential societies 3 - Processing of the collected waste into high-end products (i.e. Metals, glass, papers, and organic wastes) processed to high-end products. 4 - Improve the Nursery project and ensure the proper distribution channel of Nursery plants

Source: Buheji, M. (2018) Re-Inventing Our Lives, A Handbook for Socio-Economic "Problem-Solving", Appendix (2) AuthorHouse, UK.

4.0 Discussion

4.1 Causes of Unemployment – Synthesis from Literature

The reviewed literature shows that prime causes of unemployment can't be list under one category. Although youth don't have much difficulty about occupational immobility, they are today under a consistent challenge to learn new skills and adapt with the high speed of new industrial developments along with the change in technology and geographical immobility.

The other cause of youth unemployment is frictional unemployment which is taken by the individuals while they change their job. The literature also shows that the challenge comes from the type of approaches followed for filling the gap of youth unemployment. i.e. Youth might have seasonal unemployment which takes place due to seasonal change in the job nature as in tourism, fruit picking and hospitality. Hence, this doesn't solve the problem effectively.

Casual youth employment is a type of employment that comes in, for employees who work on a day to day basis or on short term contracts. Most of the places where casual employment exists for young people are usually based on hard labour as dockyards, market places and rarely film or tech industry.

4.2 Effects of Youth Unemployment

The literature shows the great influence of youth unemployment on the economy and the socio-economy. This is mainly because youth effects nations in their capacity for collecting tax revenues, increasing the supply cost and enhancing welfare cost. With youth being available on the job, we can lower wages, ensure the control of prices on goods and services improve the training quality vs cost, improve the living standards, increase the investors' confidence and minimise knowledge or skills drain.

The issue of youth unemployment doesn't only affect the SDG achievement, but goes further as shown from literature to affect the country's economic development, especially they are a human capital that makes one-third of the working-age population of all the emerging and developing economies. Since youth in these economies are mostly NEET, i.e. more than 20% of them are neither employed, nor in school or training, this would raise the rate of youth age in entering the market by at least three %t.

4.3 Effect of Current Youth Unemployment Policies

The reviewed literature draws on both analyses of different literature that came from both macroeconomic and microeconomic policies. Despite the diverse policies that address this issue, challenges in the youth labour market persist.

There are three major types of public policy: regulatory policy, distributive policy, and redistributive policy. Each type has a special purpose when it comes to youth unemployment. A major goal of all these policies is to maintain order and prohibit behaviours that endanger society. The policies, as shown from the literature review either try to accomplish the goal of guiding organisations towards better youth employment or engaging organisations and youth into actions that would positively affect the socio-economic and socio-political order.

Other distributive policies target to enhance the economic activities and businesses that would trigger more youth employment and create a more suitable market for them while redistributive policies would focus on promoting equality that ensures societal wealth from youth employment and capitalises on the benefits that come from such programs.

In general, once from the synthesis of the reviewed literature, one could say there is no clear evidence for approaches that are made to selecting the right policies based on experimentation or labs. With the high speed of advancement in the technology and socio-economic instability, policies seem not capable of matching the needed gap closure, especially with the slow development of the capacity of the education that meets the market demands. Therefore, testing the approaches through the effectiveness of economic policies may help the young better cope with such market disruptions.

4.4 Approaches to Inspiration Labs vs Current Approaches

The inspiration labs followed different approaches to mitigate youth unemployment as a socio-economic issue. The inspiration labs had the following two main approaches:

4.4.1 Proactive Approaches

These approaches address the distributive (the economic development) and redistributive (economic equality) policies;

as in the education for job creators and capacity building for job seekers. The proactiveness of these approaches can be either mostly direct proactive, or indirect proactive approaches.

The other proactive approaches are working on inspiring students to enhance their scientific and research contribution towards innovation index by more focused projects. The approach target to prepare youth to take more jobs relevant to scientific and research-based jobs.

One of the focused approaches that could be retrieved from the inspiration labs case study is the selective investment towards enhancing youth role in the local market and setting life purposefulness mindset that suite this initiative. The other unique proactive approach focuses on enhancing the youth employers' engagement with schools, colleges and universities and improve the youth interaction and readiness to the challenges of the local economy.

All the proactive approaches work to manage the challenges towards the transformation of self-independence and the 'big picture' legacy model.

4.4.2 Reactive Approaches

The reactive approaches work to mitigate the risks of youth unemployment and help to close the gaps of any major defect relevant to youth employment or employability efforts and preparations. The approaches here either direct reactive or indirect reactive approaches. For example, the provision of youth-focused psychiatric services that help to eliminate the negative impact of youth unemployment is one of the proactive and still reactive approaches. Same thing when ensuring that all students in under-performing school meet the minimal standard.

Part of the reactive approaches is also ensuring that all youth funded projects have made a success story and properly shared amongst youth in the labour market. In continuation of this establishing special entrepreneurship companies (using collaborative and knowledge economy techniques) for youth, migrants accelerate their preparedness for inclusion in their new labour market and eliminate their immersion in the cycle of poverty.

The strong approaches of the inspiration labs as per Table (2) is the efforts on shifting unemployment through inspiring the stratification of human capital data and building models in specific industries, as per countries sustainable socio-economy needs. These approaches also found to optimise the youth quality life through selectively targeted programs.

5.0 Conclusion

To solve the unemployment problem, we need a holistic approach that ensures the development of policies but based on experiential learning and industrial friendly approaches that accept the facts and manage to mitigate the realised risks by actual problem-solving labs and models. Such an approach could speed up the achievement of the UN-SDG regarding youth empowerment and solve the huge gap in relevance to youth unemployment. The paper shows there are many direct and indirect proactive and reactive approaches to the unemployment of youth that reached a source status and percentages in even developed countries. These approaches can go beyond waiting for decision-makers and can start from social, or socio-economic driven business models.

The inspiration labs cases listed in the table (2) show that we humans today should and could bring in more creativity to the issue of youth unemployment, through proactive and reactive approaches that could change our mindset in dealing with such complex socio-economic problem. The case study presents an opportunity for many countries and international organisations working with youth, or on the issue of unemployment, youth migration, or even youth quality of life. It is a list of approaches that might help many communities, directly or indirectly, from different perspectives on how to be both proactive and reactive regarding the issue of youth unemployment and specifically for those youth in NEET, i.e. not in education and not working.

Despite, the limitations of this study which was carried only in a longitudinal period of 3.5 years and in specific countries, the variety of approaches present many rich possibilities that could be generalised to face the coming economic downturn in both developed and developing countries. The labs presented certainly present a potential shake-up of the classical policies followed and the solution proposed in dealing with such alarming problem that hinders the current and coming generation contribution to the global development, taking that we are living in a thriving and yet turbulent knowledge and innovation-based economy. The holistic approach explored in this paper shows a new disruptive way to solving such communities' challenges, and it is certainly would open more desires for more future research.

References

Ahn, J; An, Z; Bluedorn, J; Ciminelli, G; Kóczán, Z; Malacrino, D; Muhaj, D and Neidlinger, P (2019) Improving Youth Labour Market Outcomes in Emerging Market and Developing Economies, IMF Staff Discussion Note, Jan. https://www.imf.org/-/media/Files/Publications/SDN/2019/SDN1902.ashx, Accessed on: 2/2/2019

Amadeo, K (2018) The best way to solve high unemployment according to research, https://www.thebalance.com/unemployment-solutions-3306211.

Anonymous (2108) Unemployment - Policies to Reduce Unemployment

https://www.tutor2u.net/economics/reference/unemployment
-policies-to-reduce-unemployment

Buheji, M. (2018a) Book Review- Empowering Young People in Disempowering Times Fighting Inequality through Capability Oriented Policy. Advances in Social Sciences Research Journal, 5(5) 290-291.

Buheji, M. (2018b) Book Review – 'Influence of Modern Welfare State on Socio-Economic Development', International Journal of Youth Economy 2(2),165-167.

Buheji, M. (2018c) Foreword – 'Youth Role in Transforming Change towards a better World', International Journal of Youth Economy 2(2), I-II.

Buheji, M (2018d) Handbook of Youth Economy, AuthorHouse, UK.

Buheji, M. (2018e) Re-Inventing Our Lives, A Handbook for Socio-Economic "Problem-Solving", AuthorHouse, UK.

Buheji, M (2017a) In Search of the Inspired Student—Measuring of Youth Inspiration in High School—A Youth Economy-Paper American Journal of Industrial and Business Management, 7, pp. 785-797,

Buheji, M (2017b) Investigating the Importance of 'Youth Economy', International Journal of Current Advanced Research, Volume 6; Issue 3; March; pp. 2405-2410.

Buheji, M (2017c) Forward- Youth Economy and Utilisation of Lost Opportunities, International Journal of Youth Economy, 1(2): 1-2.

Economic Discussion (2019) Suggestions to Solve Unemployment Problem.
http://www.economicsdiscussion.net/articles/suggestions-to-solve-unemployment-problem/2287

Eshelman, K (2015) Three Ways to Solve Youth Unemployment, Blog Economics, Values and Capitalism.
http://www.valuesandcapitalism.com/three-ways-solve-youth-unemployment/

European Union (2019) SALTO-YOUTH is a network of 6 Resource Centres working on European priority areas within the youth field.
https://www.salto-youth.net/mysalto/login/?pfad=%2Fmysalto%2F

Hadjivassiliou, K; Kirchner, L and Speckesser, S (2015) Key Indicators and Drivers of Youth Unemployment, Institute for Employment Studies (IES), WP3 - Policy Performance and Evaluation Methodologies, Version - 2.0, May.

Johansson, E and Handelshögskolan, S (2015) Who Makes the Transition from Unemployment to Self-Employment? Institutionen för nationalekonomi, FINLAND

KIM, V (2019) In a tough market, young South Koreans vie for the security of government jobs, Los Angeles Times, Feb 6.
https://www.latimes.com/world/asia/la-fg-south-korea-jobs-20190206-story.html

Lagard, C and Bludorn, J (2019) Unlimited opportunities: Creating more jobs for young people in the emerging market and developing economies, World Economic Forum, Feb 6.

Reddy, C (2017) How to Solve Unemployment in a Country
https://content.wisestep.com/solve-unemployment-country-best-tips/

WEF (2018) Youth Unemployment, World Economic Forum.
http://reports.weforum.org/global-risks-2018/youth-unemployment/

WEF (2019) Unlimited Opportunities- Creating more Jobs for Young People in Emerging Market and Developing Economies.
https://www.weforum.org/agenda/2019/02/unlimited-opportunities-creating-more-jobs-for-young-people-in-emerging-market-and-developing-economies-265ff21ae8/

Yahia, A (2018) Estimation of Okun Coefficient for Algeria, International Journal of Youth Economy 2 (1), pp. 1-16.

ROLE OF EMPATHETIC ENGINEERING IN BUILDING MORE RESILIENT GREEN ECONOMY

Case Study on Creating Resilient Self-Sufficient Food Security Programs in Middle East[9]

[9] Buheji, M. (2018) Role of Empathetic Engineering in Building More Resilient Green Economy. Case Study on Creating Resilient Self-Sufficient Food Security Programs in Middle East. Advances in Social Sciences Research Journal, 5(3), pp. 148-157.

Abstract

This paper targets to investigate the influence of empathetic engineering on creating more resilience economy driven government organisation structure that delivers the socio-economic needs of the stakeholders effectively. The application of empathetic engineering is carried out by the researcher for establishing a self-sufficiency program that meant to ensure food security for a middle eastern country over a period of three years. The program covered all the farms and gardens in the specified country.

The empathetic assessment helped to optimise the designing process and the integration of different jobs through understanding the best alternatives in structuring the organisation. The country benefited from establishing an integrated system and a greener economy intention that would influence the GDP and develop the country's business model in relevance to food security. The outcome of empathetic engineering is discussed in relevance on how it created more social development, causing better resilient cost centre business models that are independent of government support yet competitive and productive.

Keywords

Empathetic Engineering, Resilience Economy, Self-Sufficiency, Food Security, Agriculture Planning, Empathy Economics, National Strategies, Green Economy, Problem Solving, Behavioural Economics, Middle Eastern Countries.

Introduction

There is a growing demand for cognitive abilities for 'change agents' to recognize and understand the thoughts, perspectives, feelings, and actions of their surrounding project community and the country needs they working for. (Eisenberg & Strayer, 1990).

Through emotional empathy, emotions of others can be experienced. The optimal time to learn and practice prosocial behaviour skills such as conflict resolution and empathy responses. Recent results from brain research have indicated that parts of the brain responsible for prosocial behaviour responses in the frontal lobes.

Definition of Empathy

Early definitions of Dymond (1949) seen that empathy can be seen from cognitive perspective thus considered empathy as the cognitive ability to recognize and understand the thoughts, perspectives, feelings and actions of other individuals, organisation, community or even country. The work of Stotland (1969) sees empathy as emotional experience absorb the emotions of the other people or the environment around. Therefore, taking into account the work of Miller and Eisenberg (1988) empathy can be summarised as an influential, effective feeling that raises the ability to discriminate and identify the emotional states of the others and building the capacity to take the perspective or role of the others. This raises our capacity for the evocation of a shared effective response. Thus, empathy ensures that the perceived emotion of "feeling with" the others are perceived.

Empathy in Economics

Empathy is a subject that has interested in many disciplines, such as management, medicine, law, innovation and besides, it has its long roots in philosophy and psychology. As empathy is now being studied for its influence by neuroscientists and its research spreading through neuro-economics, it is rapidly growing as an area of economic decision-making.

Kirman and Teschl (2009) seen that both sympathy and empathy are concepts that have been used in economics at least since the eighteenth-century giving reference to Hume (1740). Fontaine (1997) was one of the earliest who established a link between contemporary economics and the practices of sympathy and empathy. Fontaine saw that sympathy works when our concerns are focused on the welfare of others, including concerns about the community. Whereas empathy works when total our capacity is diverted to put ourselves in someone place, thus to share even the thoughts of that person. However, one could experience that there is still a literature gap in relevance to empathy engineering and its role in enhancing the economic and socio-economic productivity. Fontaine (2001).

It is easy to trace the historical interest in empathy since Smith's Theory of moral sentiments which focused on how one should place his/her self in others situation by imagination. Smith see this is important for the economy since it gives us a more resilient understanding of what it would be in particular circumstances. However, empathy disappeared from the economics literature as the world lost its resilience, especially after the two world wars.

With the development of game theory, researchers started to see the essential importance of individuals interacting directly and consciously with each other, as a 'common knowledge' assumption (Binmore, 1990). Which means that the individuals involved reflect on the actions of the others with whom they interact and know that the others do the same, i.e. effectively understanding the emotions the other. Singer and Fehr (2005) called this process 'mentalizing'.

Empathetic Engineering

Binmore (1994) suggested building empathetic based models of society and its functioning based on the strategic interaction between individuals and their community. Therefore, empathy must not be considered as an essential practice that needs to be embedded in all human-related activities since it enables us to understand the nature of communication and the strategic interactions needed between all the community members and the environment around them.

Empathy, if conditioned or engineered, it would help us to anticipate other actions and contribution better accurately. Empathetic Engineering would allow the targeted individuals, organisations and communities to be resilient and strive to understand the position of the others. Therefore, empathetic engineering highly needed here in order to live and mentalize the needs and feelings of others.

Empathetic engineering, help strategic planners and human capital and organisational structure designers to create focus on what behaviour to expect from one another in order to reach a good outcome, Koppen and Meinel (2015) while the work of Binmore (1994) empathetic engineering focus on designing how to trigger the realisation of the others while selecting the preferences belonging to each person.

Empathetic Engineering and the Development of Behavioural Economics

The interest in empathetic engineering is expected to pick-up more with the continuous developments in behavioural and experimental economics, which have now started to include empathy among several other emotions attributed to prosocial behaviour, Bowls and Gintis (2003). Since empathy is taken to be a form of visceral reaction, referring to the process of changing perspective and looking at the world from another person's point of view, researchers believe that it can also be taken to be an experience of communal feelings that promotes concern for the other person's welfare.

As with the development of Behavioural Economics, Neuro-economists have now started to look at empathy applications and the possibility of its engineering in a more serious way, Singer and Fehr (2005) and Singer et al. (2006). Roughly speaking, neuro-economics tries to analyse the nature of the activation of the human brain while individuals are carrying out economic decisions or specific tasks, through different forms of typical economic experiment Fehr and Camerer (2007). Neuro-economists believe that such studies of empathetic applications will help to understand the process of how people put themselves in the place of other people.

Thus neuroscience is going to raise our ability to engineer empathetic practices and motivational reasoning. Through neuroscience, empathetic engineering would help better absorb the other person's beliefs, intentions and motivations, but to a feeling of shared experience with the other person's sensations and emotions.

The recent development of Social Neuroscience is expected to help empathetic engineering to develop further since it differentiates between the main two empathic processes cognitive empathy and affective empathy. Cognitive empathy refers to the capacity to represent other people's intentions and beliefs, while affective empathy refers to the capacity to share the feelings of others. This second type of empathy is very important for both resilience and inspiration economy since the affective sharing of a particular emotion or sensation, and experiencing the same feelings may lead to a better understanding of that person's perspectives and also influencing them indirectly.

Empathetic Engineering in Communities Problem Solving

Through empathetic engineering 'empathetic identification' can be built. This identification is crucial for human communities' problem solving, because without it equilibrium between preferences and organisational, or community's needs won't sustain. Through empathetic engineering, the interest of the community is focused and so the feelings of its needs. Thus help us to meet the national interest, or the community interest and not only someone's personal feelings only.

The unique application of empathetic engineering in problem-solving can help us see the big picture when tackling any sensitive issue that is needed for the benefit of a nation or a community. Empathetic Engineering can be applied there for solving problems in relevance to healthcare, education, engineering, etc. In this paper, building a country's self-sufficiency and enhancing its food security is investigated through actual longitudinal implementation.

Self-Sufficiency and Food Safety in Middle Eastern Countries

Clapp (2017) mentioned about the growing importance of food self-sufficiency in creating food security for many countries since the early of this 21st century. With the wake up of the international food crisis in 2007, many countries reviewed and assessed their farming and gardening practices and tried to establish a safety net from the volatility of imported food and the same time enhance the transformation towards a greener economy. This wake up was especially important for Middle East Countries and especially in countries where they are totally dependent on oil as a source of importing food from all over the world. In these countries, self-sufficiency was not part of the national plan, or even properly well stated in most of their vision.

Middle Eastern countries have been also always critiqued by economists for failure in their approach for solving food security where socio-political control the priorities of socio-economic efficiency and economic. This paper presents another way of overcoming this problem by utilising empathetic engineering in re-designing a country's farm and garden. Empathetic engineering is used here to ensure the country's security in food and its self-sufficiency.

The Relation between Self-Sufficiency, Empathetic Engineering and Resilience Economy

Most dictionaries define resilience in terms of the ability to recover quickly from the effect of an adverse incident. Therefore, in Buheji (2018) resilience economy (RE) was defined as the recovery enablers, tools and capabilities of the economy or the socio-economy to leap back. When the systems are built based on empathetic thinking utilising empathetic engineering and with a target to be sustainable by being self-sufficient, it probability of leap back efficiently is much higher.

Having a self-sufficient system means a system with the ability to produce competitive products and services, in this paper in relevance to supply of food with high guaranteed safety design to recover quickly from shocks and to withstand the effect of a shock, or even to it altogether.

Both empathetic engineering and self-sufficiency being to resilience economy the type of community that would have the mindset to be ready to unique coping mechanisms.

Methodology

Using both a country's essential need for more transformation for food self-sufficiency and empathetic engineering, the researcher has undertaken these needs as a framework for his project. Here for the purpose of the contractual agreement, the name of the country shall be Country (A). The identity of the country and the entities in the case study is not disclosed due to the sensitivity of such project to the country's security and vision of its quality of life.

The project has taken 32 months were stages of assessment, gap analysis, evaluation, early structuring, setting national strategies, setting the main team and then setting detailed organisational structuring along with communication plan.

The researcher applied the empathetic engineering in designing any structures that support the effective transformation towards more self-sufficiency without increasing the demands on the limited resources. Since food economic decision making is also very important for areas of agriculture planning, this was taken into consideration as part of enhancing country's (A) needs for more resilience economy. Resilience would be embedded as part of the researcher empathetic mindset during the process of assessment, analysis and strategic design development, about Zhang's et al. (2015).

In the Arab world specifically and developing countries in general, the creation and maintenance of such self-sufficient government and towards more of the green economy have been very bureaucratic and classical, mainly due to the hierarchical mindset that handled such specialised fields. Therefore, through empathetic engineering mindset, the focus would be on creating a resilient yet competitive agricultural industry that would ensure the supply of the country (A) secured food.

Due to the high nature of the country's total dependence on external agricultural food supply, a model was agreed to be built so that it would be both resilient and self-sufficient. Following field observations that were collected from visits to different gardens and green field in the country, it was clear that the methodologies for the types and nature of agriculture and nurseries distributed in all country regions of the country (A) need to be done in an empathetic way. When this project started, there was no evidence of an integrated and resilience in relevance to the agriculture and its contribution to the socio-economy, despite the nature and size of the farming area.

Case Study

Agriculture and Farming for more Resilient Economy

In today's workplace, the nature of how people "work together" is evolving. In resilient driven economy teamwork would transform more to be based on collaboration where the empathetic relation of people sharing the same space is expected to push them to effectively coordinate their efforts in the pursuit of stronger common goals. Today this applies even to farmers and agricultural workers who are geographically dispersed and even may never see each other, yet they are organizationally linked through telecommunications and information technologies as they attempt to achieve interdependent organizational tasks (Townsend, et al., 1998).

Such type of thinking was abstracted by the researcher with specific application to agriculture and farming business. The speed of the advances in technology, the mounting time pressure, and the demands of increasingly global and dynamic markets were all taken into consideration and blended with the empathetic engineering mindset.

Consideration and Empathy of Agriculture Industry in Arab World

Consideration of empathetic engineering in structuring agriculture industry in-country (A) would help to establish not only better communication relationship, but even better behaviours towards productivity and effective planning for food security.

In agriculture structuring, farming and gardening outcomes would be more effective if built around more resilient behaviours and characteristics that would lead to an established productive and competitive culture. This resilience in behaviours starts with having agricultural and farming teams that can assert authority without being perceived as overbearing or inflexible, while being extremely effective at building resilient communication with peers while delivering the best outcome. The ability to clarify the role of the different relationships taken by the researcher was taken in reference to the way of building passion and empathy as per the work of Jarvenpaa & Leidner (1998) and Kayworth & Levine (1998). Since country (A) target to transform more towards a green economy, unique empowerment, training and mentorship structure need to be considered. Here empathetic engineering was used again to build higher understanding (empathy) on what would exhibit a greater positive influence on the farming and gardening of team performance.

Purpose of Country (A) Project

The purpose of having structuring of all the farms and gardens that belong to the government in Country (A) was to create a holistic system of food production that would ensure effective minimum level and diversity of green food and related poultry and dairy productions, i.e. vegetables, fruits, meats and dairy products. Thus, in a way to ensure the more secure cycle of food production with more resilient management of the different resources, including the human capital and the knowledge assets captured over the years.

The project included the provision and management of animal care, beautification of gardens and palaces, requirements for gardens and farms

services delivery and all the logistics services relevant to gardening and farming protection and distribution. Grading and packaging of food and green products were also part of the services expected from these green units.

Project Assessment and Planning Stage

The project went through first a detailed assessment of what is available in Country (A) in relevance to gardening and farming versus what is really needed at this early stage towards being more self-sufficient. Based on this gap analysis, new planning based on empathetic engineering taken into consideration the needs of the stakeholders and the employees in each type of job in the system.

It is worth to mention that the project also carried the responsibility for evaluating the existence of veterinary and livestock management within Farming and Gardening responsibilities. It was as if the researcher if establishing a holistic ecosystem. Three gardens have small family Zoo's and also breading of livestock animal as Caws, Sheep, Birds, Donkeys, Tigers, Lions, etc.

The assessment using Empathetic Engineering Mindset focused directly on the strength of the Livestock Protection Unit and the speciality of a team that took care for the rare wild animals and birth control. The team were found to be very competent to meet the highest international standards for adequate sources of nutrition and hygiene with prevention from infection and transmission of diseases to humans and animals.

Analysis of Country (A) Self-Sufficiency Requirements

Analysing the requirements for service delivery of gardens and farms, using empathetic engineering again lead to suggesting the promotion of bioenergy sources (organic farming unit) as it was under demand for both the customers and to improve the quality of productions grading.

Empathetic engineering leads to pinpoint the importance of farms and garden unit that focus on Productive Capacities Management. This meant that each farm or garden in-country (A) need to be seen as an integrated cost or profit centre, where it would be given semi-independence in the management of farmers, technicians, warehouses, seasonal planning and in dealing with crises, nursery production and collaborations with nearby farms nurseries.

The analysis showed that country (A) is highly competent to decentralise each cost centre since each carried its own tools, equipment, prevention assets, veterinary services. However, the analysis showed also the country (A) really need to unify through its national strategic planning the farms and gardening goals to reach the main target of Self Sufficiency and food security. Therefore, the analysis emphasis that agricultural planning, economic production and marketing for farms and gardening need to be formulated through the strategic team is monitored and evaluated for their performance every three years.

The empathetic engineering focused on the importance of transferring and sharing knowledge from the agriculture and greenery consultants to the field engineers, farmers and gardeners. A team in the field of economics and agricultural evaluation were proposed to be formulated to ensure that knowledge accumulated by the research is transferred effectively.

Empathetic Design of Country (A) Self-Sufficiency Structure

Through a survey that was built on empathetic engineering and which included all the farms and the gardens in the country (A); the early needs for a self-sufficiency structure was identified. The survey results showed that establishing a green economic management unit (EMU) with a high authority would improve the outcome of the green production in-country (A) compared to cost enquired and would enhance green economy management, besides giving more accurate evidence of the contribution of the gardens and farms to the GDP of the economy.

The survey showed that it is important for the new EMU team to undertake intensive courses in agricultural and animal feasibility studies. A technical coordinator is required for the directorate to coordinate between the departments on issues related to economic feasibility and costing. The empathetic engineering analysis proposed further that the EMU should be supported with a legal researcher that would manage the contracts between the third parties and the directorate.

A national self-sufficiency program (NSSP) was proposed for government legislatures. The program was designed based on the empathetic engineering assessment and planning exercise carried the researcher. The proposed program was suggested to be linked to the country's vision 2030. The purpose of the legislation is to support the efforts for freeing the business model of going towards the contribution of the green economy in the country's GDP with minimal bureaucracy which the EMU team would maintain in the long run. NSSP was empathetically designed to transform the country to another less depleting resources dependent economy and reduce its dependence on external main food imports. NSSP set comprehensive performance management of green production plans for 3-5-10 years. NSSP also linked the current economic vision of 2030 to the green production output and outcome expected.

The NSSP detailed plans included the palaces most suitable as per the type of corps and the markets that it can be sold in for getting the best return and in the same time reducing or controlling the cost of the similar imported corps or food.

Through the empathetic engineering programs development of agriculture and green system found to be beyond the normal known lands, water, human capital and production economy. The researcher found that a total revamp of the irrigation system, and engineering need to be developed in a way that it would help to enhance on the return of the capital employed (ROCE), for example in the non-calculated cost of the irrigation from the wells, besides the other administrative and technical labour costs.

Establishment of Self-Sufficiency Teams

A strategic team facilitated by the researcher worked on having the empathetic thinking of both proposed EMU and NSSP as part of future references for the pragmatic model designed for the farms and garden. Temporarily a centre of planning unit is established to ensure that plans are executed with the best quality, at the best cost and with high availability. Besides, the centre was given responsibility for follow-up.

The strategic team created assignments as per speciality for the different team members as per their professional interests and backgrounds, however encouraging the multi-discipline integration. An agricultural economic planning team, was assigned to monitor the plans for environmental planning. Due to empathetic engineering, proper planning for new farms was given to the strategic team whose responsibility goes till product planning, planning for biological control along with prevention and planning for organic agriculture. NSSP included also planning for animal management and the generation of rare wild animals.

Establishing Empathetic Engineering in the System of Country (A)

In order to establish the empathetic engineering practices in the system of the country (A), Centre for Green Economy Research and Development (CGERD) was established. CGERD targets to establish empathetic engineering in all results and outcomes targeted by the strategic team and different cost centres throughout the country. CGERD was set to utilise principles of collaboration and sharing economy to ensure scientific and academic teams support effective economic projects. The CGERD is expected to take over the farms and gardens master plans updates.

Part of the efforts for establishing the empathetic engineering that takes into consideration the goal of self-sufficiency; was setting a Centre for Information Management and Quality Standards Development (CIM-QSD). CIM-QSD was established to ensure effective plants and food production and its protection information are accurate. The CIM-QSD was asked to be in charge of the procurement cost information, information technology services, livestock information, cost accounting, resource management and integration. The CIM-QSD also was given the responsibility for supervising the Technical Training Centre for Agriculture and Veterinary Medicine (TTC-AVM). This centre was given the responsibility for the assessment of the newly enrolled staff and those that go through a promotion evaluation assessment. The TTC-AVM is expected to produce comprehensive, intensive courses for new members in the different fields of specialization. A communication driven multi-disciplined program has been designed to ensure effective smooth integration of efforts and resources between all the type of farms and gardens.

The TTC-AVM was empathetically designed to support in collecting statistical evidence-based references to ensure the alignment towards the targeted outcomes. The statistics are meant to address the comparisons needs between the farms and quality of production, the best practices and the lessons learned.

Re-Designing the Role of the Agricultural Engineers based on Empathy and Self-Sufficiency

Due to the empathetic engineering assessment, the role of an agricultural engineer (AE) was promoted towards planning the season and not only supervising it. Also, the AE was given the responsibility to balance between vegetative growth and fruit growth, which in turn would enhance the country's self-sufficiency program. The AE was expected also to report about the results of the periodic examination, especially in relevance to the grading level of fruits and vegetables. This means the AE would be more accountable for the efforts taken for preparing resources in periods of land reclamation and management as an integrated project.

To ensure effective multi-disciplined self-sufficiency driven culture, it was decided that the AE would be trained by both the TTC-AVM and the CIM-QSD and later by CGERD; to calculate the annual rate and the agricultural hours and the related resources required for the next season. The AE is also expected to align the farms or garden plans with irrigation networks planned by the irrigation engineers. The AE's were given the responsibility for prepare quarterly an efficient list of the essential type supply needed as the seeds, fertilizers, and prevention medicines; besides an annual list for the agricultural equipment requiring the replacement, repair or maintenance.

Setting the Self-Sufficient Empathetic Enabler in Country (A) Business Model

In order to speed up the independence of the business model for each cost centre, be it a farm or a garden, all agriculture and irrigation engineers who have over five years were considered to part of the trainers' team. This model helps to increase the quality and type of practical training while also keeping training to be an empowerment tool and part of the annual assessment. A minimum number of training hours was enforced to be received annually for each employee.

The strategic team set a transformation team that targeted accelerating the gradual replacement of specific foreign imported green food contracts as per the defined 3-5-10 years plan. This was aligned with a program that focused on exploiting the green plants' nurseries capacity.

To define criteria for structuring the business model for any farm, the CIM-QSD agreed that farms which exceed 15 acres and have more than five wide varieties of production would have a separate cost centre. Part of the re-design of the business model is the unification of the names of each (agricultural worker) and (farmer). Both this job integration, besides the responsibility for the workers' occupational health and safety was assigned to CIM-QSD.

The farms business model included the management of by-products as the dairy which comes from farms. Hence, fresh milk and ice cream and related dairy products were assigned to CIM-QSD. This unit was responsible also for farms and garden global benchmarking, where the product and the quality of the production would be compared to similar products from different countries and even local private farms.

Conclusion

This paper carried a case that utilised different techniques in order to create a self-sufficient, food secured country. Even though this paper presents and explore the beginning of the story, it reviews and explores the possibilities that empathetic engineering brings to a complex issue as food self-sufficiency program for a whole nation. Even though the paper carries the limitation of time and space of reporting the whole case study, the case illustrates the importance of having empathetic engineering in the assessment, analysis and design in a major project that affects countries, communities and organisations.

This fundamental paper challenges different norms and assumption such as the difficulty of creating self-sufficiency in bureaucratic governments, or creating radical change in food security mindset in Middle Eastern countries. Besides, this paper shows how empathetic engineering might profoundly contribute to creating dynamic, constructive business models that bring differentiate outcome to the community, yet also build resilience economy.

References

Binmore K., Shaked A. (2010) Experimental economics: where next? Journal of Economic Behavior & Organization 73, pp. 87–100.

Buheji, M (2018) Understanding the Power of Resilience Economy. An Inter-Disciplinary Perspective to Change the World Attitude to Socio-economic Crisis. AuthorHouse, UK.

Clapp, J (2017) Food Self-Sufficiency: Making sense of it, and when it makes sense, Food Policy, Volume 66, January, Pages 88-96.

De Waal F. B. M. (2008) Putting the altruism back in to altruism: the evolution of empathy. Annu. Rev. Psychol. 59, pp. 279–300.

Decety J., Lamm C. (2006) Human empathy through the lens of social neuroscience. *Sci. World J.* 6, pp. 1146–1163.

Dymond, R. F. (1950). Personality and empathy. *Journal of Consulting Psychology, 14*(5), 343-350.

Eisenberg, N and Strayer, J (1990) Empathy and its Development, Cambridge Studies in Social and Emotional Development. Cambridge University Press.

Fehr E., Camerer C. (2007) Social neuroeconomics: the neural circuitry of social preferences. Trends Cogn. Sci. 11, pp. 419–427.

Fontaine P. (1997) Identification and economic behaviour: sympathy and empathy in historical perspective. Econ. Philos. 13, pp. 261–280.

Fontaine P. (2001) The changing place of empathy in welfare economics. Hist. Polit. Econ. 33, pp. 387–409.

Gul F., Pesendorfer W. (2008) The case for mindless economics. In The foundations of positive and normative economics (eds Caplin A., Schotter A., editors.), pp. 3–42 Oxford, UK: Oxford University Press.

Hume D. (1740) A treatise of human nature (eds Norton D. F., Norton M. J., editors). Oxford, UK: Oxford University Press.

Kirman, A and Teschl, M (2009) Selfish or selfless? The role of empathy in economics, Philos Trans R Soc Lond B Biol Sci. 2010 Jan 27; 365(1538): pp. 303–317.

Koppen, E and Meinel, C (2015) Knowing People: The Empathetic Designer. Journal of Design Philosophy Papers, Vol 10, Issue 1, pp 35-51.

Liu, W and Gal, D (2011) Bringing Us Together or Driving Us Apart: The Effect of Soliciting Consumer Input on

Consumers' Propensity to Transact with an Organization, Journal of Consumer Research, Vol. 38, August, pp. 242-259.

Oullier O., Basso F. (2010) Embodied economics: how bodily information shapes the social coordination dynamics of decision-making. Phil. Trans. R. Soc. B 365, pp. 291–301

Miller P and Eisenberg N (1988) The relation of empathy to aggressive and externalizing/antisocial behavior. Psychol Bull. 1988 May;103(3):324-44.

Ravikumar RK, Thakur D, Choudhary H, Kumar V, Kinhekar AS, Garg T, Ponnusamy K, Bhojne GR, Shetty VM, Kumar V. (2017) Social engineering of societal knowledge in livestock science: Can we be more empathetic? Vet World. Jan;10(1), pp. 86-91.

Stotland, E. (1969). The Psychology of Hope. San Francisco: Jossey-Bass.

Zhang, L; Liu, Y and Hong, J (2015) A Proposal to Support the Valuable Design Method by Redefining Empathetic Design, 3rd International Conference on Machinery, Materials and Information Technology Applications (ICMMITA 2015). file:///C:/Users/DELL/Downloads/QLTT306.pdf, Accessed: 10/1/2017

UNDERSTANDING THE ROLE OF 'INSPIRATION PRODUCTIVITY'[10]

[10]Buheji, M and Ahmed, D (2017) Understanding the Role of 'Inspiration Productivity, International Journal of Current Advanced Research Volume 6; Issue 3; pp. 2866-2871

Abstract

Productivity, be it for individuals, organisations and/or societies have been studied very closely from the point of its role in creating definitive growth in any variables it interacts with. However, still, literature is scarce about productivity that is less dependent on resources and yet lead to radical and/or sustained competitive development.

In this paper, we explore Inspiration Productivity (IP) as a new concept and investigate its ability to create a realised outcome. This paper is designed to show how (IP) help in creating productivity development towards an independent and interdependent socio-economy. Challenges towards transforming towards (IP) is discussed.

A small case study is taken in dormitory school to illustrate how inspiration productivity could change the targeted community outcome and desire to leave a legacy in life.

Keywords: Inspiration, Productivity, Inspiration Productivity, Socio-Economy, Inspiration Economy, Outcome Driven, Development, Mindset, Inspiration Currency

Introduction

In 1957, George Box proposed a "method for increasing industrial productivity" which he called 'Evolutionary Operation'. Box noted the similarities between the evolution of 'living things' and the advances in 'industrial processes', where both meet in fact that the need for consistent change (Box, 1957).

What is Productivity?

Productivity is defined as the relationship between the outputs generated from a system and the inputs that are used to create those outputs. Mathematically, $P = O / I$.

OECD (2001) defines productivity as the ratio between the output volume and the volume of inputs. In other words, it measures how efficiently production inputs, such as labour and capital, are being used in an economy to produce a given level of output. Productivity is considered a key source of economic growth and competitiveness and, as such, is basic statistical information for many international comparisons and country performance assessments. For example, productivity data are used to investigate the influence of a business model and its product and labour market impact on economic performance.

Productivity growth constitutes an important element for modelling the productive capacity of economies. It also allows analysts to determine capacity utilisation, which in turn allows one to gauge the position of economies in the business cycle and to forecast economic growth.

Mohamed Buheji

The Relation between Inspiration and Productivity

Inspiration has a unique relation with productivity since it focuses on 'pull thinking' in creating proper change. Thus, inspiration as per Buheji & Thomas (2016) creates an economy that can make productivity less resource-dependent and more of a type of opportunity creator. Through inspiration, productivity becomes selective and focused thus leads to competitiveness and differentiation. It is a principle that leads socio-economic behaviours to associate with a change in the mindset towards being active to do activities from trading to focus on abilities and capacities. (Buheji and Thomas, 2016).

Through inspiration, the main framework of productivity is shifted from being driven by (supply vs demand) to more of (capacity vs demand). Inspiration helps to have effective measures to be driven by outcome with minimal expectation reflected in what is called 'Overall Inspiration Competitiveness' (OIC).

Where OIC = Availability x Quality x Efficiency.

OIC, therefore, is a very important measure for transformation towards inspiration-based economy. OIC is a real measure of society, community, organisations and even individual ability. Through OIC we can measure the readiness to deliver the best fitness for purpose, with the most efficient and cost-effective outcome.

Since inspiration has been linked directly and indirectly for many years with job satisfaction and job performance, a positive mood, found in many studies to contribute to higher levels of productivity too (Judge et al., 2001), inspiration found to cause better productivity, especially in societies where people have more opportunities and choices. Productivity is related to the feeling of having more choices since it is found to enhance the individual's reading, debating and ability to have synthesised reflections.

Inspiration raises our ability to capture opportunities that quickly go unnoticed, or occur in areas of blind spots besides raising our precision and accuracy. The challenges, along with this more accuracy towards improving our achievement, helps to raise the spirit of persistence.

Introduction to 'Inspiration Productivity'

Inspiration productivity is multi-functional effectiveness that reflects on people's socio-economic needs or realised functional outcomes. In an economy driven by inspiration;

Inspiration Productivity (IP) = OC / I

Where, OC = Outcome that brings in Legacy

The formula of IP helps in shifting both organisations and communities from growth productivity (i.e. improve with resources and projects) to development-based productivity (i.e. improve with challenges and pull thinking influence). This is illustrated in Figure (1).

Figure (1) Inspiration Productivity Concept

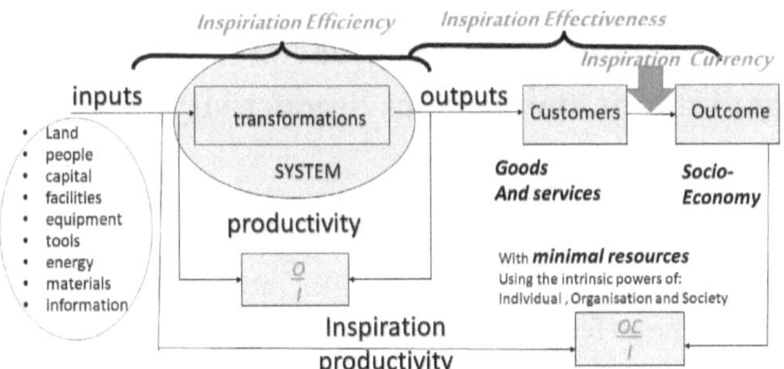

The IP is developed through the integration of inspiration spirit, inspiration opportunities and inspiration sources. This type of productivity found as per Buheji and Thomas (2016) can be delivered through experiential learning, or learning by observation and/or learning by doing.

When we come to efficiency, we normally measure it by the level of resources used to transform inputs to outputs. However, in relevance to inspiration efficiency, we would go to measure even the amount of resources used in the outcome generated. Since in inspiration-based economy, this outcome would be based on socio-economy. Therefore, efficiency in inspiration productivity is considered to be in practices as:

- Reduction of the resources actually is consumed in relevance to the outcome (legacy) achieved.
- On the input side of the system in relevance to the level of outcome achieved.
- In the measures of what the system sets out to accomplish (towards specific outcome) with what was accomplished; plan vs actual

For inspiration productivity, effectiveness is all about the outcome not only the output measure (i.e. the level of outcome – the level of quality, cost, availability, etc.).

How Inspiration transforms our organisations and societies Productivity?

Inspiration productivity (IP) is the result of managing and intervening in transformation or work processes towards the specific outcome (OC); instead, specific Output (O) only. Figure (2) shows the preferred relations of Outcome to an input to create an effective legacy.

Figure (2) Preferred relations of Outcome
to Input in Inspiration Productivity

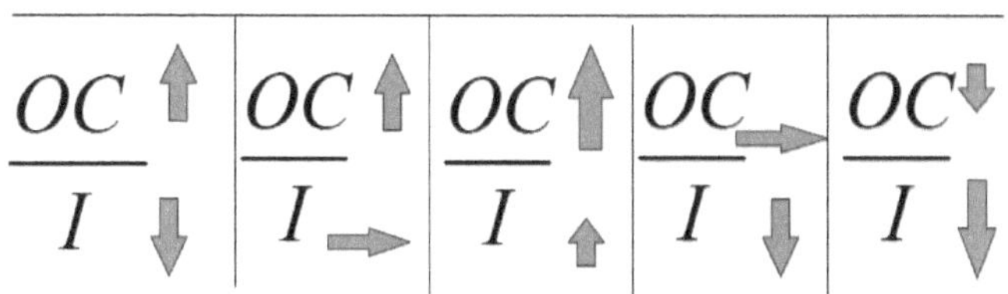

Inspiration effectiveness is about the generation of inspiration currency that leads to an outcome. The inspiration productivity measure what minimal resources were used and the use of the intrinsic powers of Individual, organisations and society (Buheji & Ahmed, 2016).

So, in summary

Full IP = (OC/I) + level of Socio-Economy generated + level of minimal input of resources used + level of intrinsic powers excited.

Productivity isn't everything, but in the long run, it is almost everything. A country's ability to improve its standard of living over time depends almost entirely on its ability to raise its output per worker. (Krugman, 1994).

Opposite to the concept of free-market economies, knowledge economy raises the ability of the organisation and the society to more useful knowledge to enhance productivity and thus creating more knowledge value-added outcome. Innovation economy, on the other hand, raises the organisation ability to create a culture of pull thinking in productivity that leads to an effective outcome. When it comes to inspiration economy, we here trying to raise the ability to discover opportunities of productivity vs level of persistence to create (legacy) and outcome. (Hübschmann and Arceneaux, 2013).

Inspiration productivity focus not only in good output, but more on building the capacity of the business model to be more towards the level of forecasting high competitiveness, as shown in Figure (3).

Figure (3) Shows the role of inspiration competitiveness in relevance to improving organisation intelligence.

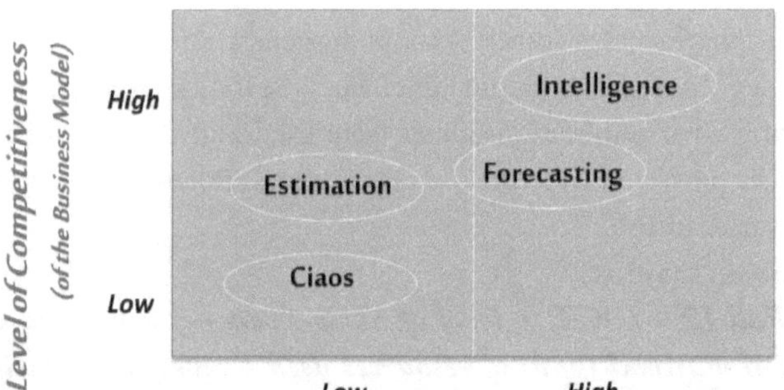

Role of Productivity in Social Development & Cohesion

Carlson (1999) mentioned that stable, sustainable economic development cannot be achieved unless and until social development also takes place. Consequently, the social dimensions of economic development and productivity are as important as economic dimensions.

Productivity and social development depend on changing human factors and targeted outcomes. Research on the social side of productivity growth and poverty reduction, for example, in developing countries by the Centre for the Study of Living Standards has largely focused on what to do about poverty and how to compensate the poor (CSLS, 2003). In inspiration productivity, the shift would be from allocating social funds to targeting anti-poverty programs that would prevent needy from being needy. It is a pro-active, positive approach to social development that aims to create a fundamental change in the business models and the community mindset again.

For inspiration productivity coexistence and competitiveness goes hand in hand. Only countries that have managed to implement and establish effective social cohesion programmes can bring about productive citizens that provide value-added to the broader community. (Marchant, 2012).

In inspiration productivity, this means we build what we call a critical inquiring mind that loves learning and has a great directed curiosity of discovering the ability to see things from an overall viewpoint. Inspiration can be studied, more and more, as part of human behavioural research. The inquiring mindset can then be linked to personality constructs such as 'openness' and 'change readiness'.

We need to re-define what we mean by growth and development, with relevance to 'value-added activities' and defined 'sustainable outcomes'. We need to structure the economy with 'value-based thinking', while taking care of productivity and ensuring the moral and qualitative value of all types of capital assets.

Development is about realised outcomes that are delivered mainly through qualitative improvements and milestones for society. If it is inspirational development, then it will be without extra resources or with minimal resources. When development occurs, our capacity develops versus demand. Thus our capacity in production would be based on fewer resources, pollution and time, or even fewer constraints of design and delivery. Thus, development is a major source of inspirational economy differentiation.

Today more papers and evidence-based books are published based on observed behaviour in relevance to social norms and preferences; including for example integrity, productivity and transparency which support the development of an established stable and sustainable socio-economic and trustworthy system. Inspiration thus can enhance the type of reciprocity that exists in our societies.

Since we are targeting a psychology-based economy that focuses on better human affairs, the framework needs to show how life is rich and colourful with feelings. This will help stimulate emotions which lead to better focused motivated productivity. It is a framework that targets to make people consistently inspired to overcome the difficulty of living choices. (Sing, 1989).

It is believed that inspiration enhances a type of productivity that focuses on "Appreciative Enquiry". This type of productivity can be a source for socio-economic revival for many non-productive and non-contributing societies.

We live in an era where focused, intelligent productivity is supposed to be much higher than before, due to the availability of technology, ease of transportation, better educational opportunities, etc. However, reports of certain developing countries' performance, especially in the last decade, indicate that they still have very low productivity per individual.

The Power of Focused Thoughts on the Development of Inspiration Economy based Wealth

Our thoughts seem to have a mind of their own, and thus we feel on many times that we are in repetitive cycles of non-productive thinking. It is possible, however, to redirect our thoughts towards a positive focus.

One of the challenges of self-initiated inspiration is the hidden costs of reward, where people already have a high interest in an activity results while they are getting less intrinsic inspiration in the long run (Frey and Jegen, 2001). Therefore, many psychologists believe that changing external instruments for inspiration help to explain monetary rewards, and regulating the use of punishment but proves to have little or sometimes even counterproductive effects.

When an organisation proceeds from maximizing its sales towards customer satisfaction, it must emphasize inspiration as an aspect of service. This would help enhance the organisation goodwill in the market besides increasing its productivity.

In his bestseller 'Competitive Advantage of Nations', Michael Porter (1988) mentioned that wealthy nations are the productive nations. Since productivity allows to support high wages and high returns on capital. We believe, however, that wealthy nations are those who can create a stable and sustainable socio-economy. If our societies are more driven by legacy creation and contribution with minimal resources, they would be even more wealthy and productive. Figure (4) shows the difference between the two types of thinking.

Figure (4) Shows inspiration productivity focused on creating higher socio-economic outcome through high hit rates

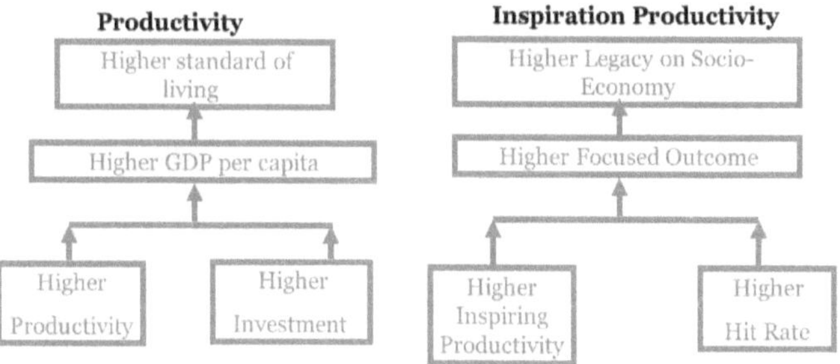

Role of Inspiration Currency in enhancing 'Inspiration Productivity.'

IP currency measures the way individuals in society respond to a socio-economy challenge. Currency targets to change the way individuals/organisations/community in society respond to a socio-economy challenge. (Buheji and Ahmed, 2016)

Inspiration labs create inspiration productivity through re-inventing business models. Through the process of inspiration, we are more able to renew business models, to be more independent & takes risks). The lab helps to make us observe interactions "humbly'. We are thus exploring and closely defining the scope while learning from interactions. The lab helps us to have better visualization, codification, classification and stratification. (Saji and Ellingstad, 2016).

Competing in both high and low-cost operating environments can present several unique challenges (Ross and Kennedy, 2014). Inspiration Productivity help to build the constructs of inspiring mindset through selective repetition.

To give an example of inspiration productivity, we take the example of a humanitarian agency called Merhamet in North of Bosnia in a city called Bihac. Merhamet was supposed to feed families in need during a humanitarian crisis. However, Merhamet ends-up committed to feeding people all year round without clear priorities to get these people out of the system and make them more independent. Through inspiration productivity program Merhamt managed in 3 months to get more than 60% of the cases.

In another can in a carpet factory in Mauritania. The inspiration productivity focused on improving the quality of life of families and their profit margin through improving the supply chain of hand-made organic products that are sold with a good margin. This let to improving the quality of life of different families and made the factory delay the focus on improving productivity through automating the factory.

This shows the uniqueness of 'Pull Thinking' in inspiration driven productivity, which is being motivated by challenging problems and gathering different ideas in a short amount of time, while viewing people and things in terms of how they can be used to satisfy needs of the community or the world.

Measuring "Inspiration Productivity" can be static where the IP=OC/I in a given time (t). And it can be dynamic: where

Index 1: IP(1)=OC(1)/I(1); IP(2)=OC(2)/I(2); then IP(2)/IP(1) yields a dimensionless index that reflects change in inspiration productivity between periods. Then, Index 2: ((IP(2)-IP(1))/IP(1))*100, yields the percentage change between Inspiration Productivity queries does not just focus on doing things better. More importantly, its focus on doing selective legacy driving things better!

Factors Affecting Inspiration Productivity.

Besides education, technology, macroeconomic policies, social and cultural environments, foreign aids and investments and industry policies & competition; other important factors affect any productivity, even at the national level. Factors as what, why, the benefits, how, barriers and trends. Other factors affecting inspiration productivity found to be the level of learning created, the well for innovation and carrying out entrepreneurial activities with independent thinking that targets to improve the socio-economy with limited resources. (Tsaousides, 2015).

At the national level, growing productivity leads to a higher standard of living that enhances our international competitiveness. At the national level, inspiring productivity leads to Quality of Life, help to create a legacy and enhance sustainable competitiveness.

There are psychological barriers to practising inspiration productivity. One of the early barriers is that we usually search for one 'right' answer. Also, we focus on being logical or blindly following the rules. This is more challenging when we become overly specialised, and we start to avoid ambiguity, fearing to look foolish or fearing mistakes and failure.

Studies, of O'Grady and Richards (2011) on inspiration in professional life, indicate that some professionals experience inspiration through (a) a sense of calling, (b) divine guidance, (c) help in solving problems, (d) a heightening of abilities, and (e) a fulfilling way of being. However, Gotsis and Kortezi (2008) seen that inspiration helps to improve an individual's relationship in the workplace by improving the overall work morale and their positive productivity that leads to creativity.

Given that workers from a vast array of professions are asserting that material gains are not sufficient motivation for productivity, and are calling for a description of organizational life that stretches beyond the metaphor of a grand money-making machine, it is reasonable to consider how organizations might systematically invite space for employees and employers to experience divine influences in their work.

Human work is a means to an end, with the end being wealth. These assumptions stem from scientific naturalism.

The worldview of scientific naturalism excludes consideration of spiritual or transcendent influences in human motivation and functioning (DiClemente and Delaney 2005).

Straumea and Vitters (2012) study investigated the idea that feeling good and functioning well-being are regulated by two different mechanisms: hedonic and eudaimonic. At the state level, it is assumed that happiness is a hedonic feeling typically experienced when life is easy, or a goal is reached. Inspiration is a eudaimonic feeling typically experienced when facing challenges in the process of goal attainment. The distinction between the two types of positive feelings also points to another interesting paradox of organizational psychology. For the last decades, the idea that the happy worker is the productive worker has been a widespread belief. (Robertson and Cooper, 2011).

Recall that deliberate practice is a crucial ingredient in developing expertise, and that the practice rated as the most important to improve performance also is rated as the least enjoyable. Judging from our results, inspiration may still be a key component in productivity even if happiness decreases because inspiration motivates people to invest energy. Turning to the practical applicability of our results, organizational initiatives aimed at increasing productivity should facilitate inspiration rather than happiness, and can do so by offering challenging and complex working environments. (Straume and Vitters, 2012).

Illustrating Inspiration Productivity in a School

In order to support the influence of inspiration productivity, the researchers carried out a small case study on a dormitory school in Cazin Bosnia. The sample was carried after the students (both boys and girls) were given a workshop about inspiration economy productivity and how they can start up a small project with minimal resources to be more independent students that create jobs or be persistent in finding better opportunities in their community.

Only 14 students fully answered the survey out of 30 questionnaires distributed. 14% of these students were above 18 years, the rest were between the age of 14 to 18 years old only. 56% of the male students mentioned that they have been working during holidays, while none of the females has had any working experience except with helping their mothers.

56% of the students said they have a goal in my life, or they know that they can work on one now. However, only 30% of them knew what inspires them. However, 65% believed that they think now that they can participate in changing their status today.

90% of the students who participated in this survey believed that now they had a lot of good information and ideas that can change their life. However, only 45% believed that they could change the world.

After taking further training, 90% of this students group believed they have started doing things that are important to their future. Actually, even 70% of them believed that now they can get more involved in practical topics that can change how people look at the role of youth in society. 30% of them they believe now that are persistent to achieve their goals and believe that if they fail, they will get up again and again.

The inspiration productivity workshop has shown to have increased the visualisation of the students in the extent of the contribution they think could give to the world. The feedback even from the school-master that this group of students started to create even more positive change with their colleagues.

Concluding Discussion

Productivity is more likely to result from appetitive feelings like interest and inspiration as a synthesis of the literature reviewed. Inspiration productivity needs an inspiring mindset that comes from critical thinking that develops the method of acting and the ability to associate things from different disciplines. This inspiring, productive mindset can be developed by the development of the 'spirit of inquiry' that help us to consistently renew our view of the world, re-define key inputs for improving decision making and make us more resilient to accept what we are questioned or challenged to.

Organisations and communities should take care of factors affecting inspiration productivity. This can be done through focusing in the creation and retrieval of inspiration currency and overcoming all the psychological barriers that prevent inspiration to flow easily.

Finally, would conclude that inspiration would stay to be a strong enhancer of unique competitive productivity that focuses on 'pull thinking' that help on being selective on what to produce and when and why to produce it in relevance to a targeted outcome and legacy. However, we need to conclude too that we need more studies in this line of the research area to support and illustrate the level of change that inspiration productivity creates.

References

Box, P (1957) Evolutionary operation: A method for increasing industrial productivity. Applied Statistics 6(2), pp. 81–101.

Buheji, M and Ahmed, D (2016) In Search for Inspiration Economy Currency—A Literature Review. American Journal of Industrial and Business Management, 6, 1174-1184. http://www.scirp.org/journal/ajibm ISSN Online: 2164-5175, Accessed:1/1/2017

Buheji, M and Thomas, B (2016) Handbook of Inspiration Economy. Bookboon. ISBN: 978-87-403-1318-5.

Carlson, B (1999) Social dimensions of economic development and productivity: inequality and social performance, Publication Type: Production Development 1 August 1999, Publisher: Defining and measuring productivity, Economic Commission for Latin America and the Caribbean (ECLAC)

CSLS (2003) Productivity Growth and Poverty Reduction in Developing Countries, Centre for the Study of Living Standards, CSLS Research Report 2003-06, Background Paper prepared for the 2004 World Employment Report of the International Labour Organization, http://www.csls.ca/reports/10-03-05_poverty.pdf, Accessed:1/1/2017

Evan, J (1999) Inspirational Presence: The Art of Transformational Leadership, Morgan James Publishing

Frey, B. and Jegen, R. (2001) Motivation Crowding Theory. Journal of Economic Surveys, 15(5): 589-611.

Hübschmann M., Arceneaux D. (2013) 21st Century Art: The Marriage of Inspiration and Innovation. In: Brell-Çokcan S., Braumann J. (eds) Rob | Arch 2012. Springer, Vienna

Judge, T; Thoresen, C; Bono, J and Patton, G (2001) The Job Satisfaction-Job Performance Relationship: A Qualitative and Quantitative Review Psychological Bulletin 2001, Vol. 127. No. 3. 376-407.

Krugman, P (1994) The Age of Diminishing Expectations. MIT Press, Third Edition.

Marchant, J (2012) In the Grand Scheme of Things: The making of inspiration through dog behaviour. FriesenPress.

OECD (2001) Measuring Productivity OECD Manual. Measurement of Aggregate and Industry-level productivity growth. https://www.oecd.org/std/productivity-stats/2352458.pdf, Accessed:1/1/2017

O'Grady, K (2011) The role of inspiration in organizational life, Journal of Management, Spirituality & Religion, 8:3, 257-272, DOI: 10.1080/14766086.2011.599148. http://dx.doi.org/10.1080/14766086.2011.599148, Accessed:1/1/2017

Porter, M (1998) The Competitive Advantage of Nations, Free Press.

Roos, G and Kennedy,N (2014) Global Perspectives on Achieving Success in High and Low Cost Operating Environments 1st Edition, IGI Global

Saji, B and Ellingstad, P (2016) Social innovation model for business performance and innovation, International Journal of Productivity and Performance Management, Vol. 65 Issue: 2, pp.256-274, doi: 10.1108/IJPPM-10-2015-0147

Sing, A (1989) Industrial Productivity: A Psychological Perspective 1st Edition. SAGE Publications.

Straumea, L and Vitters, J 2012)) Happiness, inspiration and the fully functioning person: Separating hedonic and eudaimonic well-being in the workplace, The Journal of Positive Psychology, Vol. 7, No. 5, September 2012, 387–398.

Tatebe, J (2016) Inspiration and innovation in teaching and teacher education, Journal of Education for Teaching, 42:2, 265-267.

Robertson, I.T. and Cooper, C.L. (2011) Well-Being: productivity and happiness at work. Basingstoke: Palgrave Macmillan

Tsaousides, T (2015) Brainblocks: Overcoming the 7 Hidden Barriers to Success, Prentice Hall Press.

THE DISTRIBUTION OF WEALTH — GROWING INEQUALITY?[11]

[11] Buheji, M (2019) 'Re-designing the Economic Discovery of Wealth' a Framework for Dealing with the Issue of Poverty, International Journal of Economics, Commerce and Management United Kingdom 7(2): 387-398.

Abstract

Inequality in the distribution of wealth in the globe has been growing so fast. Studies show that out of approximately eight billion world population, only 1% own most of the world known wealth. This paper investigates the possibilities of overcoming this growing inequality by examining the re-distribution of wealth.

Keywords: Wealth Distribution, Income Inequality, Resilience Economy.

Introduction

This book uses data from 21 countries to illustrate the distribution of wealth in capitalist economies that is far from being fair and equality. However, it is a book that is focused on western countries and very focused on one part of the world only.

Schneider et. Al (2016) shown in this work how wealth in this world is distributed statistically, historically and geographically.

The book explains the basics of why is the distribution of wealth important and how can it be measured, which established an important basis for the beginners and different discipline researchers in the field.

Schneider et. Al (2016) managed to show how unequal is the wealth distribution in practice and how its inequality has even changed over time. The authors have gone also into defining what factors determine the level of inequality and what are details criteria's that can be used to rank alternative distributions of wealth. The book listed the type of instruments that are available to a government that wishes to change the distribution of wealth.

Technical details as the distribution of wealth related to the aggregate amount of wealth and extent of this wealth linked to other things as economic, political and social factors; were also covered by the authors.

Current Wealth Inequality

Studies show that wealth inequality has been rapidly increasing in most world countries, since 1970. These alarming facts call for more efforts from all socio-economic leaders, practitioners, change agents and researchers; although this increase in inequality may be due that it is easier to measure and get statistics. The book tries to show alternative ways of measuring and understanding wealth, but again all from capitalism point of view. Authors try to prove that inequality has increased in recent time and with changing policies economic situation can be changed. However, this explanation is totally different from new democratic economies such as inspiration economy, the creative economy and knowledge economy which might close the inequality gap with fewer resources, by capitalizing on the different humans and society intrinsic power.

The book even though is very useful for all those who want to understand the basis of wealth in any economy, didn't consider the wealth effect from the socio-economic perspective, despite mentioning issues like inheritance, gender and ethnicity. Even though the authors explained what the actual, estimated and ideal wealth is, we believe that in reality, there are not ideal, each distribution has its positivity and negativity. Moreover, goodwill cannot be measured in measuring wealth in a normal way. The authors of the book tackled wealth from capitalism point of view and never tried to discuss the intrinsic wealth that comes from the new democratic economies as Inspiration Economy, Knowledge-Economy, Innovation Economy, Creativity Economy and even most recent Resilience Economy. We believe all these economies need to be investigated in relevance to exploration and distribution of wealth too.

Conclusion

Even though the book has technical details and lots of tables that illustrate the historical changes that could be presented more friendly non-economists using diagrams of infographics, the authors managed to emphasised their perspective of unequal distribution of wealth through such statistics. It is worth finally to say that Schneider et. Al (2016) team shown clearly how affluence and well-being depend only on the fraction of the social cake, as it depends on the social area. We believe that this book carried distinguishing statics that links between risk and distribution of property, besides other important information on the dynamics of wealth in relation to GDP.

References

Buheji, M. (2018) Re-Inventing Our Lives, A Handbook for Socio-Economic "Problem-Solving", AuthorHouse, UK.

Buheji, M. (2018). Recognising Lives around Socio-Economies? – Foreword, International Journal of Inspiration & Resilience Economy, 2(2): 0-0

FINAL WORDS -
KEEP VISUALISING BETTER
RESILIENT COMMUNITIES
LIVELIHOODS

Similar to our needs to secure the basic necessities (food, water, shelter and clothing), we need more than ever today to build resilient communities' livelihoods which have a set of approaches that help us to manage the challenges and be tolerant to a sudden crisis. Communities livelihood involves the capacity to ensure sustainable and continuously developing activities that overcome turbulent economic, ecological, and socially complex contemporary or foreseen situations.

Having intolerant communities that refuse diversified life is a serious socio-economic problem that might lead to both socio-environmental and socio-political problems which deteriorate our livelihood. Therefore, we need to tackle non-resilience as an issue of hidden opportunities that need to be exploited until we reach optimum resilience status.

In this book, we started to tackle different non-resilient modalities, by reviewing the destruction of capitalism, the economics of climate change and the uprising of new economic concepts, such as sharing economy. The editor focused the intention of the reader towards these issues to help in smoothening the transformation towards 'resilient-communities'. Then, approaches and mechanisms of resilient communities are reviewed to help mitigate any coming socio-economic crisis. As an example of these approaches is the mitigation risks that would help to build resilient communities in dealing with youth unemployment, was presented.

The book shows that resilience of communities can be more mature with optimisation of empathetic engineering, inspiration productivity and ensuring the effective distribution of wealth that close the inequality gap between the different levels of the society.

Finally, resilient communities work on balancing opposing values. They bring in, for example, the value of humility and audacity. Such communities depend on the development of self-realisation that keep them focused on facing complex problems that would lead to lasting social impact.

KEYWORDS

Mitigation of Risks, Empathetic Engineering, Resilient Communities, Outcome-Driven Communities, Distribution of Wealth, Poverty, Inspiring Productivity, Self-Sufficiency, Empathetic Thinking, Empathetic Engineering, Proactive Approaches, Reaction Approaches, Socio-Economic Problem Solving, Inspiration Labs, Inspiration Economy, Socio-economic Crisis, Resilient Mindset, Resilience Development Opportunities,

BRIEF ABOUT
DR MOHAMED BUHEJI

Dr Mohamed Buheji is the founders of the International Inspirational Economy Project and Institutes. He is *considered a leading expert in the areas of **Inspiration, Excellence, Knowledge, Innovation, Inspiration, Change Management and enhancement of Competitiveness** for over 25 years.* *He is a retired professor from the University of Bahrain. Besides being* **a Future Foresighter.**

*Dr Buheji is also the **Founder of the International Journal of Inspiration & Resilience Economy and International Journal of Youth Economy.** He has published since 2008 more than 70 peer-reviewed journal and conference papers and 17 books in the subject of the **power of thinking, lifelong learning, quality of life, inspiration and competitiveness**. Also, he has **five books in English about Knowledge-Economy, Inspiration Economy, Inspiring Government and Inspiration Engineering, Resilience Economy and Youth Economy.** He is passionate about transferring his + 500 consultancy projects experience for more than 300 organisations from all over the world, to both education and research.*

*Besides, Dr Buheji serves in the editorial board of 5 internationally peer-reviewed journals. He is a member of many scientific communities, journals, academic review boards. Lately, he is a winner of many awards including the latest **CEEMAN best*** *researcher award for 2017,* besides being a **Fellow of World Academy of Productivity Science.**

Address: International Institute of Inspirational Economy, P.O.Box 37313, Bahrain [e-mail: buhejim@gmail.com, web site: www.buheji.com]